Game Changer

How to Thrive When Life Doesn't Go According to Plan

By

Sam Kuhnert

GAME CHANGER

Ordering Information:

Quantity sales. Special discounts are available on quantity purchases by corporations, associations, and others. Orders by U.S. trade bookstores and wholesalers.

DREAMSTARTERS

www.DreamStartersPublishing.com

Table of Contents

Introduction

A Better Dream

If you'd have asked me ten years ago what I wanted to do with my life, I would have told you, "I'm going to be a major league pitcher." It was a worthy goal, sure, but it was also my only goal. If someone would have told me then that my dream of playing major league ball was never going to happen, I would have been devastated. I wouldn't have believed you if you told me a better dream would eventually come my way. Back then, being a game changer meant playing professional baseball and only playing professional baseball. Proving to myself and to everyone else that I could do it was the one thing I wanted the most. I set my sights on becoming one of the few major leaguers to play with one hand like my heroes Jim Abbot and Pete Gray. It was the only real dream I'd ever had and, let's be real, it was a selfish one. I loved God and I read my Bible, but, back then, I was all about what He could do for me. Not what I could do for Him. I wanted glory and recognition and the power that comes from being famous. I had an idea of what my life would look like and that picture was pretty self-serving. I saw myself playing in the majors, doing a little charity work on the side, maybe marrying the perfect baseball wife and having sons, but basically basking in the limelight of being a professional athlete as much as possible.

I didn't know then that another dream—a bigger, better dream—was coming. One that would blow my self-serving vision for my life right out of the water. I didn't know that I could live a life of deeply satisfying purpose until I had a vision of how God wanted to use me. It was both thrilling and terrifying, and I knew I needed to step out in faith. I didn't give up my dream of becoming a baseball player; I added a new dream alongside of it and, over time, that new dream blossomed into the main event. With this new dream, I began to realize a greater purpose that wasn't only about me. It was about so much more.

I'm going to take a guess, since you're reading a book about being a game changer and living a life of purpose, that maybe you're looking to make some changes in your own life. Maybe an old dream crashed and burned, and you need a new one. Maybe you've never had a big dream for yourself and you want to know how to find one. Or maybe you need some inspiration to do life differently. You want something new or something bigger or maybe just something unlike what you're doing today. You might need encouragement to help your child, another family member, or a friend. You might not be limb-different like I am, but we've all faced challenges and we all have our own baggage and issues to overcome You might simply be in a place where you're having a hard time believing that things can be different for you—that you even have a purpose—and you need some hope. You need someone to tell you that you can do it.

You can.

I believe that God has a purpose for you. No matter what your life is like right now or what it was like in the past, God can use everything you've been through and everything you are to make your future totally new. Want to know how I know? Well, for starters, listen to this:

Last summer, 179 limb-different children and their families came to a camp in a small town in rural Illinois. They came from all over the world to spend a week with me and my fellow coaches so they could learn how to play sports, develop their skills, tie their shoes on their own, and make new friends for life. This was just one camp. Over the course of the last several years hundreds of children have been to camps all over the nation. And it happened because I allowed God to gift me a bigger, better dream than anything I could have come up with on my own, and to take control of my life. I became willing, and He put in motion an adventure that has been so much more satisfying than playing in a major league game ever could have been.

Today, my purpose is to dream with God and chase after those dreams relentlessly. It's about being a game changer and choosing to live my life everyday intentionally pursuing my purpose with every choice I make, every opportunity I take advantage of, and the people I surround myself with. And, at its core, it's about helping people. Because of all the things God has done, so many kids with limb differences can learn courage and confidence through sports from coaches like me who are also visibly different. Because of our camps, Samuel, born in China with no lower legs or hands can compete in wrestling and basketball. Because of our camps, Will, a middle school baseball player who lost his arm to cancer, learned how to play with one hand and enjoy the game he loves again. Because of our camps, Ella, born with a nub just like mine, kills it as a leader and starter in every school sport she plays. These are just three examples out of a thousand.

I don't tell you these things to brag. I tell them to you to show you that if the class clown ball player from the middle of nowhere can get the opportunity to do something so fulfilling and so affirming, you can too. Your dream and your purpose will likely look different than mine, but it won't be any less amazing. Any less fulfilling. And any less impactful. Let me tell me you a little bit more about myself to give you the full picture:

I was born with no left hand, simply a nub where my palm would be and five small nubbins instead of fingers. I spent years of my life hiding my nub in my pocket because I was ashamed and afraid. I was ashamed of how God made me, and I was afraid of what the other kids would say to me—because over the years, both kids and adults said awful things to me. I spent many other years being a bully to smaller kids because I was tired of being the one who was always bullied. And when I wasn't doing one of those things, I was doing one of two others:

- Practicing Sports
- Goofing Off

And when I say goofing off, well, I might have been the perpetrator of some . . . let's call them incidents . . . during my youth. For example, do you know what really gets people excited at the beach? I once thought it might be fun to pour ketchup all over my nub while I was partway out in the ocean. And then I raised it in the air and started screaming, "Shark! Shark!"

You want to see people get out of the water fast? It was definitely one of my more effective pranks. My mother was so proud, let me tell you. And that's just the tip of the iceberg. I've done a lot of things that most people would think were "cool," but that I'm definitely not proud of. Things I would be tempted to take back if I could.

I share this with you to show you that you can live a life of meaning and purpose no matter who you are or what you've done. If you feel like you've missed your chance or lost your dream, I'm here to tell you, a better dream is coming. And you can live it. I know you can.

I'm going to walk you through twelve key practices that have transformed my life. Don't worry. It's a process. It doesn't happen overnight. You don't have to have it all figured out today. You don't have to do all twelve things by Tuesday. You don't even have to know all twelve things by Tuesday. Today, all you have to do is decide and believe.

Decide that you can and will live a life of purpose.

Believe a better dream is coming. Even if you don't know what it is yet.

Make a decision today, and then take a step forward. Tomorrow, take another. You'll be amazed how a willing heart and a decision to do something will change your life.
I believe in you, and I know you can do it.

Let's get to work.

Sam Kuhnert

Chapter 1
Accept Who God Made You to Be

Life Is More Fun When You're Friends With The Person In The Mirror

---

For we are God's masterpiece. He has created us anew in Christ Jesus, so we can do the good things he planned for us long ago.

Ephesians 2:10 nlt

You never forget your first bully's name.

It doesn't matter if you haven't seen him in twenty years or if you have long since moved on and up in life. You remember the name, the face, and worst of all, the way that person made you feel. I've had a lot of bullies, but the first one's name was Mick. He was bigger than me—tall and stocky—and he had a mullet. If you grew up in a small Midwestern town anytime between 1970 and 2005, it's likely you've seen at least one bully with a mullet.

I was four the day I met Mick and he brought an unsettling reality to my attention—I was not like everyone else.

"Hey, gimme that Megazord." My friend Trent and I were playing together on the first day of preschool. We were rolling a ball back and forth when Mick interrupted.

"Here you go," I said as I turned to hand him the Power Ranger Megazord, not knowing I was about to meet my own personal villain.

"What happened to your hand? Where is it?" he asked without a single ounce of concern or kindness in his voice. "Is that thing going to grow back?" I looked down to where my left hand should have been. Where there should have been a hand, there was a nub. And where there should have been fingers and a thumb, I had only five small nubbins.

"I don't know," I said, "I don't know where my hand is." Until that moment I thought I was like everyone else. It never occurred to me that I was different or that something was wrong with me.

I went home from school that day and climbed the stairs to the room I shared with my older brother. I crawled into my bed, stared out the window, and cried my eyes out. This would be the first of many days and nights during my childhood that I spent crying in my room.

My mom came up to see what was wrong, and I asked her, "Why, Mom? Why would God make me this way? Will my nub ever grow into a hand?"

My mother is the kindest, most gentle person I have ever known. And though I know now that her heart was breaking at my words, she calmly sat down next to me and rubbed my little four-year-old head. She didn't teach me to be mean or to get even. Rather, she encouraged me to look to God.

[[callout: I praise you because I am fearfully and wonderfully made; your works are wonderful, I know that full well. —Psalm 139:14 niv]

That day began the first of many conversations with my mother where she would motivate me, support me, and tell me that I was perfectly made by God. I am not perfect, but I was fearfully and wonderfully made in His image. God didn't make a mistake. He had a plan and a purpose for me I could not yet imagine.

The day I was born did not go exactly how my family expected. My parents had no warning that something might be amiss with the pregnancy or the baby boy my mother was carrying. My family spent the weeks and months after my birth dealing with a measure of fear instead of experiencing the total joy and celebration they had anticipated. It was especially hard on my dad. He's always been an outdoorsman and an athlete. He kept thinking, how will I teach my son to play baseball? How will I teach him to cast a line or shoot a bow and arrow? He worried that people might not accept me; and he was concerned how this might affect my spirit.

My grandpa kept wondering, how will he tie his shoes? It's likely that my shoes weren't really chief on his list of concerns, but somehow the ramifications of what life would be like for his new grandson with one hand were distilled simply to this one question.

Friends, relatives, and a lot of people in our community were praying for us. My grandparents had spent a few days wringing their hands and worrying about what life would be like for me when their minister showed up at their front door to encourage my family.

"Dianna," he said to my grandma, "I need to tell you something. I've been praying for Sam, and I want you to know that God has a plan for him. Sam is going to be a blessing to his family, and not only to his family, but to the world."

[[callout: "Sam is going to be a blessing to his family, and not only to his family, but to the world."]]

12

In that moment my family released a breath they'd been holding for days. God brought them hope in their darkness, and they knew it was going to be okay. They might not have known how I would tie my shoes, but they began the journey of accepting that God made me perfectly, and He had a plan for my life.

As I grew, I was much like other little boys—the ones who are all boy—into everything, rough-and-tumble—and often faster than their poor mamas can keep up with. While I don't remember the first time someone put a ball in my hand; it quickly became a permanent fixture. All I wanted to do was play ball—much to the chagrin of all my other toys. Once I started throwing my tractors like they were baseballs, people stopped giving me tractors.

When I was less than a year old, my mom left me with my older brother in the sand box for approximately two seconds when she turned around and found me climbing up the TV antenna on the side of the house. That was the day my parents took a collective sigh of relief. Together, they put their fears to rest. (Their fears about my missing hand, that is—I think they might have discovered some new fears, like me falling off the side of the house.) They knew hard times would come, but they also knew their boy was going to be more like other kids than they had imagined.

Home was a safe place for me when I was little—I could play ball and be encouraged as I grew to do what everyone else was doing. The men in my family are outdoorsmen and athletes. My dad started helping his dad on the farm at five years old and was a farmer for 50 years. I didn't realize I was different because my parents were so intentional about finding ways for me to participate in the activities our family loved. My parents were also intentional about not enabling me. They made sure I was loved and nurtured, but they didn't let people do everything for me, and they certainly didn't let people say, "But he can't." They believed that I could, so that's what they told me, thereby creating an environment that fostered my independence.

Being surrounded by people who believe in you and tell you that you can is what I like to call a game changer. Not only did my parents tell me that I could, but they taught me, supported me, and expected me to do just about everything for myself. If all the people surrounding you are telling you that you can't, you might need to find some new people. Wisdom and caution are wonderful—but constant negativity and total lack of belief and expectation—no thanks! If you want to be able to accept who you are and how God made you, ask God to fill your life with the right people who will believe in you.

It wasn't until I went to school—specifically until I met Mick—that I realized I was different. Once a fearless, happy toddler, I suddenly became a self-conscious little kid. The second I discovered I could hide my nub in my pocket, it disappeared. Keeping it hidden was my goal.

Struggling to understand why God made me this way and why I wasn't like everyone else often exacerbated the pain of dealing with stares and snide comments until it all became more than I could handle. I hated that I was different, that I didn't have two hands like everyone else. On the days I came home and cried, I couldn't see past my pain in the present moment. What little kid could?

Mick tormented me nearly every day of preschool. And though I went home and cried myself to sleep every night, I didn't want the other kids to know it hurt me. Forming a tough exterior I decided to fight back. Instead of using my words, my nub became a billy club. Unafraid of the reprimands from my teachers, I lashed out at everyone who tried to mess with me. If a bully was going to say things about me, he was going to pay for it. Standing up to my bully provided a small sense of relief, but the feeling when I returned home remained the same.

If you're facing challenges or painful experiences I want you to know it's okay to be scared. And it's okay to feel sad and even angry. Sometimes hard things happen to us, and in our humanness, it can be difficult to look out beyond our pain, beyond our circumstances, and beyond the scope of our lives. It's our nature to focus on ourselves, especially when times are hard. Especially when you're a child.

What a blessing it was that I had a family who refused to let me be alone in my sadness, who helped me on the journey to accepting myself each step of the way. My mama read Scripture and Bible stories to me every single day. She taught me that we don't have to stay scared and we don't have to stay stuck. It's okay for a season, and then it's time to look up and look out. But before we look out, we must first look in the mirror.

The First and Most Essential Practice

The first and most essential practice I needed to develop in order to move on from the pain and into my purpose was simply to like myself and accept the way God made me. The Creator made me perfectly in His image. I don't need to be ashamed. I don't need to hide away my nub. I can't control the past; but I can accept the present.

It doesn't matter what our struggle is. You may be physically healthy, whole, and complete, but your confidence is non-existent. Perhaps anxiety and fear control your life. Or you don't feel like you are smart enough, strong enough, rich enough . . . fill in the blank.

I'm here to tell you that you are. You are enough. Exactly as you are. God made you perfectly in His image, and He wants you to know that He loves you and is working all things together for your good. The first step toward moving forward is accepting that God made you, and he has a plan for you. A good plan.

[[And we know that in all things God works for the good of those who love him, who have been called according to his purpose. —Romans 8:28 niv]]

15

My first practice centers around what I like to call the three strikes. People think strikes are a bad thing, and they are, unless you are the pitcher. Then strikes are the best thing! When you drive off the mound, putting your whole self into the pitch and you watch the ball zoom into the catcher's glove, there is no better sound than the thump of a baseball hitting leather and the umpire's voice shouting, "Strike!" Just like I had to practice to throw strikes in baseball to become an effective pitcher, I had to practice throwing these strikes too:

Strike one: Accept yourself. Look into the mirror and for once, let the shame, guilt, or fear roll away. This is easier said than done and often won't happen overnight. As I noted, like a pitcher has to practice and develop, you, too, will need a regimen of coaching yourself into this practice.

First, arm yourself with Scripture and other positive promises. I have an arsenal of them:

I will praise You, for I am fearfully and wonderfully made;
Marvelous are Your works, and that my soul knows very well.
Psalm 139:14 nkjv

I can do all things through Christ who strengthens me.
Philippians 4:13 nkjv

The Lord appeared to him from far away. I have loved you with an
everlasting love; therefore I have continued my faithfulness to you.
Jeremiah 31:3 esv

For we are his workmanship, created in Christ Jesus for good
works, which God prepared beforehand, that we should walk in
them.
Ephesians 2:10 esv

But blessed is the one who trusts in the Lord, whose confidence is in him.

Jeremiah 17:7 niv

Jesus replied, "Truly I tell you, if you have faith and do not doubt, not only can you do what was done to the fig tree, but also you can say to the mountain, 'Go throw yourself into the sea,' and it will be done.

Matthew 21:21 niv

Read these to yourself over and over again, until you are almost sick of them. Eventually, the truth of those words will be emblazoned on your heart, and you'll believe them. You'll look in the mirror and realize you have truly accepted yourself. The person staring back at you is perfectly created by God and full of potential.

Strike two: Practice confidence. I know it seems like people are either born with confidence or they're not, but the longer I live, the more I know that's not the case. Sure, some people might be born with a greater measure than others, but I think confidence has a lot to do with our experiences and our environments. And like anything else in life, if we want to become good at something, we have to practice it.

The first step to practicing confidence is studying it. Look around at the people in your life. Who has genuine confidence? Be careful here not to mistake confidence for arrogance. A lot of people put so-called confidence on display, but it's often a defense mechanism full of arrogance. Here are a few ways to tell the difference:

Confident people are secure, and those who possess both of these qualities are kind. They don't need to put people down to feel better about themselves or step over others to get where they are going. They celebrate others' successes. In general, a confident and secure person isn't going to be mean, passive aggressive, or shame

17

people. You might meet an arrogant bully, but you won't meet a confident one.

Another important trait of confident people is that they don't tend to obsess about what others think of them. For one thing, they're too busy living their lives and using their gifts to spend the time worrying about what other people think. For another, they don't care. Sure, they probably want to make their moms proud and be good employees and good spouses, but there's a difference in wanting to be well thought of and respected and worrying too much about what everyone else thinks.

Confident people believe that they can. They work hard and they have high expectations for themselves. They take measured risks and get up each day putting one foot in front of the other. They do things sometimes simply because they believe they can.

Know people in your life like this? Hang out with them. Ask one to mentor you. Become their friend. And then put some of these things into practice:

Be kind.
Stop obsessing about what other people think.
Believe that you can.
Now hold your head up and get to it.

Strike three: Speak life to others. Your story starts to come full circle when your life becomes a blessing to the people around you. When you finally reach a place of security with yourself and with God, then you can bring encouragement to people. Proverbs 18:21 nkjv says, "Death and life are in the power of the tongue." We can speak death over people or we can speak life over them. Plenty of people tried to speak death over me. Coaches told me I couldn't. Kids were just plain mean. Secure people speak life, and it can be a game changer for those who are struggling. Where would I be if my mother hadn't spoken life to me, day after day, year after year? Who do you need to speak life to? If you are a parent, your kids need it. If you are married, your spouse needs it. If you're a human, pretty much everyone around you needs it.

[[callout: Death and life are in the power of the tongue. — Proverbs 18:21 nkjv]]

I know it's hard to believe that how we see ourselves—how liking ourselves and accepting ourselves—really matters, but it does. And it matters in ways we can't even imagine.

When I was about 11 or 12, one of the opposing coaches on my travel league reached out to me for the first of many times. He gave me a VHS copy of a television movie that was made in the 1980s called A Winner Never Quits, and it was about the life of a man named Pete Gray who played baseball in the 1940s. This moment changed my life in several ways. For one thing, it made me aware of another limb-different major league baseball player. And Pete wasn't just missing his hand; he was missing most of his right arm. Until he lost his arm as a child, he had been right handed; he then taught himself to be a one-handed, left-handed ball player.

The movie made me feel like the coach must have really believed in me if he thought I needed to see this—it made me wonder if maybe he thought I could be like Pete, and I could make it to the big leagues too. Knowing he believed I could be a winner helped spark a flame of confidence inside of me. I have never forgotten that he did that, and I have never forgotten about Pete.

Watching this movie and learning about Pete Gray's life taught me another important lesson. It showed me what's really at stake when it comes to accepting yourself—and it also made it very clear to me that accepting myself and liking the person God made me to be had to be separate from my accomplishments.

When our boys came home from the war in 1945, Pete got sent back down to the minors. He played there until 1949, and then he went back to his small hometown in Pennsylvania.

Pete did some amazing things in his life beyond playing major league baseball. He visited veterans in the hospital after the war to encourage amputees.1 When he was back home, kids always came to him for his autograph, and he was always quick to give it and treat them at the local candy store. Unfortunately, he also struggled with drinking and gambling during parts of his life, and he spent much of his life in poverty. He never married or had children.2

There's certainly nothing wrong with not marrying and living a quiet, humble life, but various interviews and reports suggest that Pete struggled. An article in the Chicago Tribune said, "Overcoming his physical handicap apparently was easier for Pete Gray than finding a so-called inner peace."3

I can see how easy it would be to make things look okay on the outside while holding onto the struggle on the inside. As you'll see in the coming chapters, I would carry that same struggle with me for many years. I was angry, and I was afraid. I never wanted anyone else to see those things—to see how I really felt and who I really was.

Thankfully, I figured out that I didn't want to do that forever. I didn't want to spend my life in a state of angst, alone and afraid of getting close to people, angry over my circumstances, and always worried what everyone else thought. I wanted to be comfortable with who I was—I wanted to like the person God made me to be. And thank God, now I do.

I don't want you to have those struggles either. Your struggle might look very different from mine, but whatever it is, I hope you look yourself in the mirror every day and begin the practice of accepting who you are and liking the person God made you to be. Nothing on earth feels as good as peace with God and peace with the person he made you to be.

I'd like to think that Pete eventually found what he needed and was able to do that too. I'll know I'll always be grateful for him.

Chapter 2

Make No Excuses

Hanging Onto Our Excuses Isn't Going To Get Us Where We Want To Go

---

"Mighty hero, the Lord is with you."

Judges 6:12 nlt

I have distinct memories of sitting in my dad's lap while we watched Jim Abbott play baseball. Jim was a major league pitcher during my childhood who also only had one hand. I remember being perfectly tucked in next to my dad in his recliner. He'd lean down and say, "See what he did there? See how he transferred his glove?"

I soaked in everything. Every pitch. Every catch. Baseball became my dream. And I knew that if Jim Abbott could do it, then I could do it too. I couldn't wait for my turn.

My brother Charlie is four years older than me, which means he got to start playing baseball first. When his games were over, I ran straight onto the field. My dad and my brother's coach always let me practice afterward. They pitched to me and let me practice pitching. I remember many Midwestern summer evenings when small crowds would gather and watch the little boy with one hand play ball under the lights on the baseball diamond.

I loved baseball with every fiber of my being. And I loved having a crowd watch me, but even then I remember wanting them to watch me because I was good. Not because I only had one hand.

22

I realized from an early age I was going to have to outwork everyone else. And I knew I'd never be able to make excuses. [[callout: I knew I'd never be able to make excuses.]]

My parents instilled into me the habit of no excuses at a very young age. If we want to live a life of purpose, we can't go around making excuses about everything. This one is big, and this one is hard. We live in a culture where it is easy to make excuses and easy to blame others. Don't do it. Don't give in to that pressure.

Excuses are a dime a dozen and nearly everyone has one. Or five. Here's the thing: some of them might actually be legitimate excuses, but it still doesn't matter. Please hear me on this. I'm not trying to be unsympathetic. Trust me, I've worked with some amazing kids who have overcome incredible odds. And if anyone had the right to make excuses, it would be some of them. I say this because I know that hanging onto our excuses isn't going to get us where we want to go. When we are more committed to hanging onto our excuses than moving on and living a life of impact, well, that's where we'll stay. Hanging onto our excuses.

I can't tell you the number of people I've met whose excuses have been coddled, nurtured, and allowed to become bigger than their drive to achieve. I've met people who hide behind their disabilities, hardships, families, upbringings, and myriads of other things to justify why they can't do something.

I don't get that at all.

Why wouldn't we want to succeed? Why wouldn't we want to work hard and accomplish something great? Something worth remembering? Whatever you do, don't feed your excuses!

I've seen so many people use their disabilities as an excuse to get out of things or to keep themselves from being pushed to do more and achieve at a higher level. Their families have babied them;

they were allowed to quit when things got hard. Or they're scared they'll fail and they hold tight to any reason not to get in the game since they can't fail if they don't try. I played on teams that I hated, but my parents never let me quit or not give 100%. That taught me a lot about commitment and sticking with the hard stuff—it started the long process of developing my character and sense of integrity. I didn't like it at the time, but I'm a better man because of it. Whatever your difficulty is, be bigger than your excuses.

[[callout: Be bigger than your excuses.]]

I don't say any of this lightly. It's hard to let go of our excuses. Sometimes it's hard to even recognize them, and it can be easy to slip into them without even realizing it. Be alert in this area and ask people who are close to you to help you. From my experience, I think there are three keys to living a life of no excuses, and the first one involves being surrounded by the right people.

Make sure you have people in your life who can tell you no. Remember my grandfather's fear when I was born? "How will he tie his shoes?" Well, it ended up being an actual issue. I couldn't tie my shoes for a long time. But I had a friend who always helped me. He was there for me and tied my shoes for me. And then one day, when we were in the fourth grade he came up to me and said, "I'm not tying your shoes for you anymore."

This friend had always helped me. At school. During games. On the playground. When we played basketball, if my shoe came untied, I'd call time out and either he or one of the refs would come and tie my shoes. It was kind of embarrassing; I'm not going to lie. But I only had one hand, and I couldn't tie my shoes. It was a weak point for me, and I needed him. Or so I thought.

So out of the blue, this nine-year-old who was apparently wise beyond his years informs me that he's not helping me anymore. And here I am, stuck, because I can't do this most basic thing. I couldn't exactly call my mom onto the basketball court to tie my shoes in the middle of the game. I had no choice but to learn to tie my shoes. And you know what? I did.

By telling me no, my friend did me a huge favor. Sure, eventually I probably would have learned to tie my shoes. But because of him, it happened a whole lot sooner. This leads me to the second key:

Persevere. Persevere. Persevere. Whatever you do, keep trying. Keep going. And don't give up. Do you know how many times I had to practice tying my shoes? I assure you, it was ridiculous number of times.

A coach at the school where my mom taught had a huge impact on our lives. He was just like me and was born with only one hand too. I'd go to his classroom after school and he'd try to show me how to tie my shoes. His help was invaluable; though I ended up changing the way I did it just a little. This man would continue to be a positive influence and a source of confidence in my life for years to come.

One night after my shoe-tying lessons, I went home and practiced for hours. I sat at the island in our kitchen, tying my shoe over and over and over again. Can I tell you what a celebration our family had when I finally got it? It was like I had won a championship game.

Now I realize, when it comes to things people have to overcome in life, shoe tying isn't that big of a deal. But the principle applies. What we do with the small things will also apply to the big things. And for someone with one hand, small things can certainly feel like big things—learning to tie my shoes, learning to type in high school, and learning to tie a tie in college. (Many hours of YouTube were watched for that particular endeavor.) And when I was little, and I decided I was going to be a baseball player? I had to try a lot harder and train a lot longer than most kids just to figure out the basics of how to throw and catch a ball.

[[callout: What we do with the small things will also apply to the big things.]]

I'd like to think that's the spirit of a winner inside me . . . but it might just be my bullheadedness. When it came to baseball, I had to practice so much more than everyone else. I threw a ball up against our shed so I could practice my glove transfer, catching, and fielding. Over and over and over again. I did this for hours and hours a day and for days and days on end. One of the best gifts I've ever received was a pitch-back net. I was thrilled! I could continue my practice, and the net was so much more effective than the side of the shed. My parents were probably just trying to keep the shed from falling apart, but, for me, it was a huge new tool in my arsenal. I kept pushing. I kept practicing. I kept going. And you know what? I became a baseball player.

The third key is the most important of all. You'll need it on the dark days. The ones where it's so tempting to reach back to your excuses. The ones where you don't have anyone around to tell you no, and especially the ones where you have tried so hard for so long, and you still don't seem to measure up. The third key is this:

Remember that the Lord is with you. If you take nothing else away with you, take this. The Lord is with you. One of my favorite stories from the Bible beautifully illustrates this point.

"If the Lord is with us, why has all of this happened to us?" nlt

I can relate to the man who asked this question. I trust God—at least most of the time. But sometimes it's hard not to ask why. Why, God? If You are with us, why did this happen?

I've asked this question while crying alone in my room. I've asked it standing on the pitcher's mound, and I nearly always wonder about it after receiving biting remarks from insensitive people. In desperation and frustration, when I feel as though I have persevered as much as I can and yet have continued to fail, I hang my head and ask God why.

About three millennia before I came around, an Israelite named Gideon asked this question. Gideon lived during a time when the Israelites were making bad choices, and the Lord handed them over to the Midianites. One day, Gideon was threshing wheat and trying to hide it in a winepress to keep it from the Midianites. The Midianites were a cruel people. They were so cruel that the Israelites hid themselves in the mountains and caves to be away from them. If they planted crops, marauders would attack Israel and then destroy all the crops. Then they would take all of the animals and livestock. The Bible says that so many enemy hordes descended on the Israelites, they were "as thick as locusts; they arrived on droves of camels too numerous to count" (Judg. 6:5, nlt). Can you imagine what it would have been like to see an enemy like that descend upon you? They stripped the land bare and reduced the Israelites to starvation. So the Israelites cried out to the Lord for help.

In the midst of this utter desperation, Gideon is trying to hide wheat, and the angel of the Lord comes, sits under a tree, and says to him, "Mighty hero, the Lord is with you" (Judg. 6:12, nlt).

This is what prompted Gideon's question. A question that nearly all of us ask at some time or another: If the Lord is with us, why?

Why is this so hard?
Why did this happen to us?
Why was I born this way?
Why can't I figure this out?
Why me, God? Why?

Sometimes it seems that there is no end to our whys. We know God is good. We know He is faithful. He has helped us

27

before. But when it feels like we are trapped in our desperation, our circumstances, our depression, our fill-in-the-blank, it's so easy to forget. Gideon knew God had brought his ancestors out of Egypt. He knew miracles had been done on their behalf. But now? Now he felt abandoned.

I've never faced starvation or marauders of any kind. I have certainly never been under that kind of attack. And my enemies? Our enemies and our trials might look very different, but at some point or another, we've all felt alone. Like Gideon, we're pretty sure God is with us, but we still feel abandoned. We're sick, or scared, or lonely, or no matter what we do or how hard we work, it seems we'll never be able to move forward.

Based on the rest of the conversation between Gideon and the angel of the Lord, I have to wonder if he was thinking, a. Why is this happening to us? and b. I'm sorry, did you call me a hero? The angel then goes on to tell him to go with the strength he has and rescue his people from the Midianites.

If I had been hiding in cave on the side of a mountain, starving, and witnessing my people's utter destruction by a cruel and terrible enemy, I think I'd first look over my shoulder to be sure he was actually talking to me, and then I'd be stumbling in confusion, disbelief, and fear. "I'm sorry? You think I'm a mighty hero and you want me to do what?"

Gideon asks how he could do this because not only is his clan the weakest in the entire tribe of Manasseh, but he is the weakest in his whole family.

I know that feeling.

God, how can you use me? I'm the weakest. God, how can you use me? I only have one hand.

"I will be with you," the Lord told Gideon, "and you will destroy the Midianites as though you were one man."

[[callout: "I will be with you," the Lord told Gideon.]]

Gideon could have made a lot of excuses. The temptation to do so would have been incredible. He asked for confirmation, and he asked for signs, but then he got up and did what the Lord asked him to do. Step by step, he followed the Lord's instructions until he had exactly what God wanted him to have to defeat the Midianites—an army of a mere 300 soldiers.

Gideon first gathered with 32,000 men, but the Lord told him there were too many—if He gave them a victory over the Midianites, they would boast that they had won by their own strength. He told them to tell anyone who was afraid they could leave, and 22,000 men went home.

Then the Lord told him to let the men drink from a spring and separate the men who lapped up the water in their hands from the ones who knelt down and drank from the spring. He wanted him to keep only the men who drank from their hands . . . that left him with 300. And the Lord said, "With these 300 men I will rescue you" (Judg. 7:7, nlt).

Before Gideon went into battle, the Bible says that he bowed and worshiped the Lord. That's an important reminder for me. It's His strength we rely on, and before we step out into any type of battle, we should stop and worship Him.

What happened next was epic. I think it's one of the most awesome scenes in the Bible. Not only has Gideon thrown aside his excuses and followed God into what must have been a terrifying pursuit—there were 135,000 Midianites—but he must have also instilled some amazing confidence in his men. He told them to keep their eyes on him and do exactly what he does when he does it. Each man had a torch in a clay pot and a ram's horn. When Gideon and the men with him broke their jars and blew their horns, all 300 men followed suit. They smashed their jars, raised their torches, and shouted, "A sword for the Lord and for Gideon!"

That almost gives me chills. Bravery, dedication, and obedience all came together in one mighty roar. When the men did this, massive chaos ensued, and the Lord caused the Midianites to panic and kill each other. God gave Gideon the victory that night, and for the rest of his life, the Israelites lived in peace.

We can sit with our excuses forever, but like I said, that will only leave us with our excuses. And remember what God said to Gideon? If He let that many men fight, they would boast? If we were perfect, if we came from a different family, if only we could.. If we were or had all of those things, would our accomplishments be about us or about God? Who would get the glory?

We may never fight that particular kind of battle, but each of us has our own battles to fight and win and all of them are important to God. So whatever it is you're fighting for, whatever it is you want to be—don't make excuses. I know it's scary out there. The enemies can be terrifying. But remember, my friend, the Lord is with you. And when we're brave enough to step out with our weaknesses, the glory ends up going to God, where it belongs.

Chapter 3

Don't Let the World Get You Down

The Only People Who Can Decide What You Are Capable Of Are You And God

---

"It's hard to beat a person who never gives up."

Babe Ruth

Baseball was and is a tradition in my house like Thanksgiving is a tradition. It comes around year after year with much anticipation. It is savored and celebrated. It makes us nostalgic for the past and hopeful for the future all at the same time.

In my world, we had two seasons—winter and baseball season—and every year, I couldn't wait for the winters to end. Some years, we started practicing when it was still snowing, but spring and summer would finally come. In the small towns and open fields of the Midwest, you can see the lights and smell the hot dogs from miles away. Even still today, the twilight blue sky on warm summer nights fades to navy and voices ring out, "hey batter," while small crowds gather to watch the games.

Growing up, baseball was my constant. Do you remember the scene in Field of Dreams where James Earl Jones walks onto the field with the ball players from history and looks at Kevin Costner and reminds him that throughout all the years, baseball has been America's constant? He's trying to convince him to not sell the field

31

and the farm, even though he's up against tremendous risk. He's urging him to remember that baseball is the thing that reminds us of what was once good and could be again. He's trying to help him have faith against all odds.

I had a lot of people like James Earl Jones in my life. In fact, I would say I had more people like him, people who believed in me and wanted to help me. But I also had people like Kevin Costner's annoying brother-in-law in the film. Well-meaning, perhaps, but constantly negative. He might have had good intentions, but he had no faith, and all he could see was how and why things were never going to work out. It's hard to drown out those people, even if they are fewer in number.

We were at the ballpark all summer, every summer. Some of my favorite memories happened under those lights. And so did some of my worst.

❖

Cut Like Mike . . .

For decades, cut and jilted kids everywhere have been comforted with the words, "It's okay, Champ. You'll get 'em next year. I mean, even Michael Jordan got cut from his high school basketball team." It mattered not what the poor souls got cut from—basketball, swing choir, the spring production of Fiddler on the Roof—these were the words of comfort extended for any and all quasi-related circumstances.

And, you know, that sentiment would have been really inspiring . . . except that he didn't get cut. He just played JV as an underclassman instead of varsity. Could have been a great story if it weren't for that minor detail.

My turn to get cut and hear the trademark "Michael Jordan Words of Comfort" came around when I was in the seventh grade. I was finally old enough to try out for the school team. I was going to wear my uniform proudly and represent my hometown. Long before tryouts rolled around, I had been playing and practicing really hard. I was so confident in my tryout. I just knew I was finally going to be a DuQuoin Warrior.

It's funny how some memories stick with you. I'm a grown man, and I remember the feeling I had when I read that roster and my heart dropped to the pit of my stomach. I remember it like it happened yesterday.

My mom had just driven me into town for the Friday night football game; I loved going to football games. Coach said the roster was going to be posted on the school doors, so we went by the school to confirm the good news. I jumped out of the SUV and ran to the list. I read it. I read it again. And again. Each time, my name continued to not be on the list. And my heart dropped like a rock.

I had played for that coach on travel teams for years. I was never one of his favorites, but I was one of his consistently good players. I was absolutely stunned. I got back in the car and asked my mom to take me home. For the rest of the weekend, while my aunts and nanas were coming out of the woodwork to comfort me, wrap me in awkward hugs, and of course, remind me that even Michael Jordan got cut, I couldn't help but think about every time in my childhood I had overheard someone at the ballpark say, "Do you think this kid will be able make it to the next level?" And the dreaded answer that always came, "No, nah, I don't think so. This will probably be it."

No, I decided, this will not be it.

Victory often feels like a long, slow climb where you take two steps forward and one step back. Or sometimes, two steps forward and then you fall flat on your face, dust yourself off, and

33

start climbing again. It's like running the 110-meter hurdles. You clear that first hurdle, and it feels so good until you realize you've got nine more to go. Every time I cleared a hurdle, there was still something else to prove or someone else to show that I really could play ball, and that it didn't matter that I only had one hand.

[[callout: Victory often feels like a long, slow climb where you take two steps forward and one step back.]]

I started playing baseball before I was actually old enough to start playing baseball. If my brother's team didn't have enough players, I was there. On the field and ready to go. Then I finally got my turn to play tee ball and then play in the leagues where the coaches pitch to little kids. The coaches would lob it up to me, like they were trying to be more gentle or something, but I hated it because not only was the ball harder to hit, but also because it made it more difficult to hit the ball hard. Nobody thought I'd make it past that league—for some reason it didn't matter that I could hit and field better than most of the other kids. It's like that nub was a flashing neon sign that screamed to people I was incapable . . . and yet the reality was, I was totally capable. It was so frustrating.

After the coach-pitch league, I made it on to kids pitch. Amidst doubts and fear, I was even able to be a pitcher. I wanted to pitch so badly, and I'm sure my parents had a measure of fear letting me go out on that mound, but they let me do it anyway. Everyone seemed to be afraid I wouldn't be able to make the glove transfer quickly enough to field the ball and defend myself. In baseball, the pitcher controls the game, but the pitcher is also the most vulnerable. A hard shot up the middle can be dangerous with two hands. Every time the coach asked my dad if he was sure it was okay that I pitch, he confidently assured him it was. And I got to go step out on the pitcher's mound, which to me was the happiest place on earth.

Tee ball, coach pitch, kid pitch, travel ball—on and on I went even though so many people were sure I'd never make it to the next level. And then I got cut from the seventh-grade team.

It took awhile, but I picked myself up from that cut in the seventh grade, worked unbelievably hard, and then got cut again the following year. It was incredibly demoralizing. My parents continued to support me. I played travel ball. They hired a trainer to help me; I'll never forget the day the trainer, who was an assistant coach for a nearby community college baseball team, looked at me and said, "They cut you from the team?" It was so affirming, and at the same time, so maddening.

Finally, I made the team in high school. I was both relieved and excited—I had finally made the team. I had been working so hard; I knew there was no way they wouldn't put me on the mound and throw me.

I was wrong.

After all of my training and all of my success on the junior legion team, I only got to pitch three games out of about 25 that year. And the funny thing was, every game my coach started me on the mound was a game he was certain we were going to lose. The first team that I pitched against was set to destroy us, and I got the 1–0 win. In fact, I won all three games against teams that were supposed to beat us.

The next year was some more of the same, but I got to pitch a few more games, and I got to bat a little more. No matter what my coaches said or thought, I wanted to keep going, to keep moving up, and to keep playing ball.

One beautiful spring Saturday during my sophomore year, we were playing a doubleheader against one of our rival schools, the Herrin Tigers. So many things about that day were perfect: it was 70 degrees and sunny, I was surrounded by family and friends, and I was playing baseball. During the second game, I stepped up to the plate.

I knew the catcher on the team; he was a good guy and a good athlete. We'd seen each other play, and we were both the biggest boys on our teams. Before I got into my stance, he called time and ran out to the mound to tell the pitcher something. After the game, he confessed that what he'd ran out to tell him was: "Do not throw this kid a fastball."

The thing about cocky, teenage pitchers is that they're not great about being told what to do or not do—especially if those instructions suggest their fastball isn't fast enough. He didn't listen, and that first pitch was one of the most beautiful I had ever seen—a fastball right down the pipe—and when I swung that bat I did something I'd dreamed of doing since I was a little boy sitting on my daddy's lap watching ball games on TV.

I hit that ball so far it soared over the high fence in left field, over the concession stand, and onto another field. This is what I'm told; I didn't actually see it. I put my head down and ran so fast I was rounding second and on my way to third before the ump finally caught my eye as he swirled his finger in the air to signal the home run.

It was the most incredible feeling.

I got to home plate, and my teammates were waiting for me to pound me on the head and slap my back. I looked up and saw my mom in tears. Then I realized that just about everyone in the bleachers was in tears. It was funny, for being an away game, so many special people in my life were there to see my homerun. My parents and grandparents and even family friends who weren't typically at my games were there that day.

I know I got to grow up in a pretty special town, because that was more than a decade ago, and people still approach my parents and me about that homerun. Sometimes even strangers come up to us to say they were at the field that day and remember seeing my homerun. A sweet older man we've know for years still says, "Sometimes I just lie there and think of Sam's homerun and it puts a smile on my face."

That moment was so amazing, and I wish I could tell you it turned the tide for me and opened the door to more playing time, more at-bats, and more success. That was not the case, and I didn't bat again the rest of the season.

My junior year started well. I was primarily a relief pitcher, and I was brought in a lot to give our team a chance to win. I thought I'd finally cleared the hurdles, but then one day after pre-season workouts, I stopped to talk to the pitching coach. I was feeling pretty good about my arm. I approached him after practice one day to talk through some things. I wanted to know what I needed to work on to keep going; I wanted to know if he thought I was good enough to play at the college level. He quickly told me I was not. "You are throwing hard, but there aren't too many one-handed pitchers that make it that far. These four years of high school will be it for you. Just enjoy them; I don't think you can make it in college."

The Key to What You Can and Cannot Do

The key I learned throughout this process is an important key to keep in mind both when people are telling you that you can't do something and when they're telling you that you can do anything.

The key is this: the only people who can decide what you are capable of are you and God. That's it. It's great to have encouragers. It's so important to have people who speak life into you and help build your confidence, but in the end, it's you and God who decide.

[[callout: The only people who can decide what you are capable of are you and God.]]

I'd love to tell you that you can do anything, but the reality is, you probably can't. I, for example, am never going to play basketball like Michael Jordan played basketball, nor is anyone going to ask me to paint the ceiling of the Sistine Chapel. Or any other ceiling for that matter, unless they'd like a nice, flat white rolled on. I think we were all born with certain passions and gifts, and the degree to which we engage ourselves with them and work hard for them, is the degree to which we will succeed as God allows us to.

[[callout: I think we were all born with certain passions and gifts, and the degree to which we engage ourselves with them and work hard for them, is the degree to which we will succeed as God allows us to.]]

It's possible that that coach was watching my speed and thinking, Nope, he's just never going to make it past high school. But how much different would my day, my season, and possibly even my high school career had gone if he'd said, "You know, Sam, I'm not sure. I'm not sure if you've got enough speed on your fastball to make in college, but you know what? Here's what we can do. Here's what we need to look at to help you improve and try to get you to the next level. . . ."

I didn't want him to lie to me or blow smoke; I wanted honest feedback, but I would have preferred it come with some dedication and help. That moment gave me my greatest coaching lesson, and I use this all the time when I'm helping kids. I learned that both truth and faith need to work together, and they need to be served with a big side of dedication. When kids come to me with those questions, I either reassure them that, yes, they can do it, or I tell them I'm not sure, and I work out a plan to help them or get them the help they need to succeed.

[[callout: Truth and faith need to work together, and they need to be served with a big side of dedication.]]

Over the years, I had some amazing basketball coaches. They didn't shower me with fluffy, "you can do it" praise. But they stayed after practice and worked with me. They pushed me hard, both literally and physically. Sometimes we did post drills, one-on-one, and they did not hold back. I had to get tough or get knocked down. It didn't matter what drills we were doing in practice—I had to do what everyone else did, and I was not allowed to make excuses. I was mandated to figure it out. It was so hard. And that was so amazing. They believed in me. And because of their belief, they worked extra hard to help me, and they raised the bar extra high for me.

My dad was the same way. My dad's arm was a cannon, and when we'd play catch, he'd fire that ball back at me so hard so I could train my reflexes and build muscle memory. When I pitched, if I threw a wild pitch, he'd let it go and tell me to run and get it. "You don't want to run? Then throw strikes." My dad was a huge part of my success; he showed me where and how I needed to grow, he kept me humble, and he stayed right there with me to help with all of it.

No matter who you run across in life, remember, you and God decide how far you're going to go. Practice believing this. And while you're at it, when you're in a position of influence and authority, don't give the people under you any guarantees other than the guarantee that you're going to help them achieve their absolute best.

When you have the opportunity to be James Earl Jones or the annoying brother-in-law, always be James Earl Jones.

Chapter 4
Work Hard

And Know Why You're Doing It

Winners embrace hard work. They love the discipline of it, the trade-off they're making to win. Losers, on the other hand, see it as punishment. And that's the difference.

Lou Holtz

When I was 14, my dad bought a 1961 Massey Ferguson tractor the color of rust. He spent about $400 on the thing and told me I had a new job. If I wanted a truck of my own someday, I was going to have to earn it.

We hauled that giant hunk of junk into the barn and got busy restoring it. I'll never forget the day we started sanding her down:

"Dad, can I use your electric sander?"

"Nope."

I was confused.

"Here you go," he said, as he handed me a sheet of sandpaper. "Get to work."

I was 14. I had no idea why I, in the modern era of power tools and electricity, was sanding a rust-covered tractor that was older than my father by hand. I just wanted a truck. My dad isn't exactly the kind of guy you say, "Nope," back to, so I picked up the sandpaper and started sanding. And sanding. And sanding.

Don't get me wrong; I had the persistence of a dog with a slab of ribs. I kept working, but I also kept asking. I was not letting it go . . .

"Hey, Dad," I'd say as I looked up from a tiny shiny spot on the tractor, "Look what I did. Can I get the sander now?"

He'd lean in to check my work. "Nah," he'd say, as he smiled and handed me another sheet of sandpaper.

Eventually, I started to pick up on some things. Perhaps this was about more than a truck. Perhaps I was here for some life lessons. And lesson number one was that even if I didn't think I had what it took to get the job done, I had to keep going and keep working hard anyway.

As it turns out, that's how most of life works. We've got a dream, a goal, a need—work to do—and we don't have the thing we think we want—or need—to do it. Sometimes we've got to use whatever we have in our hands and get to work anyway.

[[callout: Sometimes we've got to use whatever we have in our hand and get to work.]]

Piece by piece, I kept sanding that tractor by hand. The little shiny spots grew and grew until finally, I had sanded about a fourth of that tractor with what felt like a million little sheets of sandpaper. And then one day, my dad handed me the sander.

I'm not sure what the experience would have been like if I'd always had that sander. It sure would have gone faster. It would have been a whole lot easier. But then Dad and I wouldn't have been able to talk as much over the hum of the sander. My arm certainly wouldn't have been as strong. I might have missed out on some really important moments. Maybe my dad wasn't being difficult just because he could as much as he was teaching me what it means to be a hard worker. To get the job done. No matter what. Somehow he must have known I was going to need that.

You see, even though I was clueless in the beginning, I had a couple things that kept me going:

I wanted a truck.
I trusted my dad.

That's it. I wanted a truck, and I knew I could trust that my dad was a man of his word. If he said there was a truck on the other side of this nonsense, I believed him. It's amazing what we can accomplish when we have a strong enough why and a reason to believe something.

[[callout: It's amazing what we can accomplish when we have a strong enough why and a reason to believe something.]]

Baseball was the love of my life. I worked and worked and worked at that sport, harder and longer than all of my teammates. I loved it so much, it hardly bothered me when I missed out on trips to amusement parks, concerts, and camps with my friends. I didn't even care because I was hard at work at my passion. And I had to develop the habit of working hard if I wanted to be one of the best. And that was the thing. I knew I'd never make it if I didn't keep working. I knew if I stopped, there'd come another day where my name was not on the list, and I'd be ushered off the field for good. I loved nothing more than being on that ball field, so I kept going. Hard work might be one of the most important habits we can develop to be game changers. Let's talk about the keys that make hard work meaningful and possible.

First, here's a big fat disclaimer: hard work is not glamorous. You've got to be disciplined, you've got to sweat—figuratively and sometimes literally—, and occasionally you're going to hate it. At times people are going to make fun of you. Others won't believe in you. And you'll likely have moments where you feel like you might not believe in yourself. But I'm telling you, don't miss out on it. Thomas Edison once said, "Opportunity is missed by most people because it is dressed in overalls and looks like work." How many people in the world don't even know they have amazing, God-given talents because they are not willing to do the work? How many opportunities are slipping by us because we're not willing to pick up the sandpaper?

Here are three things that have kept me working hard when it would have been easier to give up or not even start in the first place:

The Why. I kept sanding that rusty old tractor because I wanted a truck. I had a strong enough why to keep me going when it was hard, sweaty, and awful. The same was true for baseball. I wanted to keep playing, so I kept working. Having a strong enough why gives people a reason to accomplish amazing feats. It's one of the reasons men and women give their lives for their country—they have a deeply rooted why that drives them, even to the ultimate sacrifice. It's how people scrimp and save and live on the bare minimum to pay off extreme amounts of debt—they have a why and a goal that is driving them forward. It's how the healthiest and most successful athletes stay healthy and successful—they make good choices with their bodies and with their lives, because it's not worth losing their dreams and all they had worked for to partying and a few fun nights.

Necessity. Goals. Dreams. Your why might be any number of things, but you've got to have one. And then you've got to keep your eye on the prize and move forward. When it gets tough— because it will—you can remember why you are doing it, and it will help you press on another day.

[[callout: But one thing I do: Forgetting what is behind and straining toward what is ahead, I press on toward the goal to win the prize for which God has called me heavenward in Christ Jesus. — Philippians 3:14 niv]]

If you're feeling a little lackluster about life or if you're struggling to work hard at things, stop and ask yourself if you have a why to help drive you. It can be easy to fall into routines and go through the motions sometimes. Without a why, you can become apathetic without even realizing it. Trust me, I've been there. Having or not having a why to drive you can be the difference between being a game changer or merely drifting through life and missing beautiful opportunities.

If you don't already have your why, I'd encourage you to spend some time thinking about what it might be. It might be what you need to get through some hard days until you land that dream job or until you make it through that class you hate. It's easier to do that when we have a love or passion for the work that needs done, but sometimes we need to persist even if we don't like something. Finish. Work hard and do well. Keep going until you get to the other side. Here are a few questions to ask yourself to help you figure out what your why might be:

1. Write down five things you're passionate about. These can be activities you love doing, ministries or causes that are meaningful to you, people you love being with, a dream or major goal you have.

2. What do you most enjoy doing in a given week? Think through what it is you're doing when you feel the happiest and the most at peace. Now what do you need to do to spend more time doing that thing or being with those people?

3. Where do you want see yourself in five years? What do you need to do to get there? Could you take a class, read some books, or meet new people who could mentor you? Write it all down.

Figure out what your why is and then grab hold of it with both hands and make a plan. You might not find yourself sanding a tractor or throwing a ball up against a shed at all hours of the day and night, but the next time you're working hard and wondering what on earth you're doing it for, think of your why—that goal, that dream, that plan—smile, and keep working.

The Belief. The second thing you need is belief. Belief in yourself and belief in something far greater. Belief can be an incredible driving force to keep us working and moving. When it came to that old tractor, I believed my dad. I believed in who he was, and I believed that what he told me was true. And when it came to baseball, I believed in myself and I believed God made me capable enough in spite of my limb difference.

Before you start to doubt yourself or think about all the reasons why you can't do something or shouldn't believe in yourself, I'm going to stop you right there. You can. You really can do it. The bestselling author Stephen King once said that talent is cheaper than table salt. That's pretty cheap. He went on to say that what separates the talented individual from the successful one is a lot of hard work. The good news is that if we feel like we just don't have enough talent, it doesn't actually matter. Talent is not the deal breaker. Instead of worrying about talent, think about all the reasons why you can do it and why you should believe in yourself. Here are some verses that encourage me when I need it:

Fear not, for I am with you; be not dismayed, for I am your God; I will strengthen you, I will help you, I will uphold you with my righteous right hand.

Isaiah 41:10 esv

For I know the plans I have for you, declares the Lord, plans for welfare and not for evil, to give you a future and a hope.

Jeremiah 29:11 esv

When you walk, you won't be held back;
when you run, you won't stumble.

Proverbs 4:12 nlt

When you doubt that you can do something, spend some time thinking about others who've accomplished incredible feats or who have overcome unbelievable odds. Think of people who have worked hard.

One of the most familiar stories in the Bible is about a man named Noah and his ark. Noah was born a mere ten generations after Adam. In the scope of history, that was not long at all. In Genesis chapter 6, the Bible tells us that the Lord saw that the wickedness of humankind was great in the earth and that it grieved Him to His heart. Humans were behaving so badly that God was sorry that He'd even made people. In ten generations, the world became almost completely full of violence and corruption. And just when God was ready to destroy everything, the Bible says, "But Noah found favor with the Lord" (Gen 6:8, nlt).

The Scriptures go on to say that Noah was a righteous man who walked in fellowship with the Lord. And because of that, God made a plan to save him. But it wasn't going to be easy.

I think sometimes we gloss over this story without really thinking about just what God was asking of Noah. It's the story on the cover of Bible storybooks for children and the mural on the walls of church nurseries. It's fuzzy animals and pretty rainbows, right?

Well, not exactly.

Imagine with me, for a moment, the following conversation with God:

God: I've decided to destroy all living creatures on the earth. People have filled the world with violence.

Noah: (Silence.)

God: I want you to build a large boat, 450 feet long, 75 feet wide, and 45 feet high. I'm about to cover the whole earth with a flood that will destroy every living thing that breathes.

Noah: (Silence.)

God: Enter the boat with your family and bring a pair of every kind of animal with you and keep them alive during the flood.

Noah: (Silence.)

In Genesis chapter 6, as God is telling this plan to Noah, Noah never actually responds. The very last verse of chapter 6 simply says, "So Noah did everything exactly as God had commanded him" (Gen 6:22 nlt). Can you fathom how much work that had to have been? The ark was enormous. It was 90 feet longer than a football field, including the end zones! And Noah didn't have a forklift or a power saw. He couldn't drive to Home Depot to buy 2 x 4s or nails. He had to make and build every piece of that ark with his own two hands and a limited set of basic tools. Forget sanding half of a tractor with sandpaper, this was hard work like you and I will never know.

The Bible doesn't tell us exactly how long it took Noah to build the ark, or really even much about the process. I know it would probably take you or I years to build an ark like that. I wonder what it was like and what he thought about while he toiled away during those sweaty, back-breaking days in the sun trying to complete an overwhelming amount of work. I imagine there were times where not a single cloud broke the blue expanse of the sky overhead, and a flood seemed impossible. We don't know exactly what Noah was thinking, but we do know that he finished and that he finished to God's specifications, exactly as requested.

Not only did Noah have to save himself and his family from the flood, but the fate of the entire human race rested on his work and obedience. Noah had a why, a reason, to keep working. But more than that, he must have had a deep, deep sense of belief. He was a righteous man who trusted God. If he hadn't believed in who God was and what He said, how could he have ever kept going?

About a year after that old tractor landed in our barn, after we'd taken every piece apart and put it all back together again—rust-free and covered in a new, shiny coat of red paint—my dad sold it for a whole lot more than he paid for it. That profit was the down-payment for my truck. Together, we'd worked hard. My why pushed me forward, my belief paid off, and though in some ways I was sad to see it go, that tractor got me my first truck, just as promised.

Whatever you do, don't be afraid of hard work. It's one of the most deeply satisfying parts of the human experience.

In the next few chapters, we're going to talk through a few more key practices in the lives of game changers. Anger, fear, and pride are all common emotions and experiences that we all face at some point. Like hard work, what we choose to do with them is what sets us apart—or not.

Chapter 5
Use Your Anger for Good

Let's Funnel The Right Kind Of Anger And Our Energy Toward Making The World A Better Place

---

"It is wise to direct your anger towards problems—not people; to focus your energies on answers—not excuses."

William Arthur Ward

Hurt people hurt people.

This is true no matter how old you are, but it's a lot more obvious when you watch kids. Kids are still learning how to process emotional pain, so they are a lot more likely to lash out when they've been hurt. That was definitely true for me. Having only one hand made me a prime target for teasing and bullying as a kid, and all of those mean words hurt. It took a long time and a lot of growing up before I could really explain why I was so angry all the time. Everyone tells you to ignore bullies or people who hurt you, shake off their words, and move forward. I tried to do all of that, but it's much easier said than done when it comes to forgiving and forgetting emotional pain.

One night, after one of my sixth-grade basketball games—a good game, where I'd scored a lot of points and played well—I had an experience that cut me to my core. I lined up with my teammates to shake hands with our neighboring rivals, and rather than receiving fist bumps, high fives, and "good games" instead I heard:

"I'm not shaking that thing."
"Ewwww, gross!"
"Don't let it touch you!"

And not one single player on the other team shook my hand.

Back then, I couldn't figure out if what those kids said hurt the most, or if it was the fact that not one single player or coach on my team did or said anything to defend me. Now, as an adult, I know that it was their silence that made the other team's meanness unbearable. The team's cruelty was awful, but my friends' and coaches' silence was deafening. I expected teasing and taunting from strangers, sad as that is to write down, but I didn't expect silence from the people who were supposed to be on my side. I kept it together until I left the locker room, but the second I was in the car with my family, I broke down and bawled my eyes out. My parents and grandparents didn't know what to do or say, but I know their hearts were breaking with mine.

Weeks went by, and no one at school ever said a thing to me about the incident. It had been shoved under the rug, or so I thought. And then one day, my mom ran into Rhonda, my friend Trent's mom, at the ballpark.

Trent was one of my best friends who also happened to be one of my silent basketball teammates. We hadn't talked much in the last few weeks after that miserable game. We'd both been busy with school and sports and honestly, I'd been avoiding talking to my teammates after what happened because I was so hurt and embarrassed I didn't know what to say. That year, Trent and I were playing on different travelling baseball teams. Trent was a great pitcher, and for as young as we were, he could throw the ball really hard.

Funny thing, eleven-year-olds don't always know how to process and articulate hurt or anger. And eleven-year-old boys aren't always great about talking about their feelings. Who knew, right? Sometimes, they just do the best they can. Turns out, when that team made those cruel remarks, I wasn't the only one who got upset. Trent got mad. Really mad. And when he took the mound against a baseball team filled with the boys from that mean basketball team, he used his fastball to show them just how ticked he was. He beaned almost every single player he recognized from the basketball game, starting with the boy who'd made fun of me first, and then he made his way down the lineup. Trent wanted to teach those boys a lesson, and they knew exactly why they had bruises after going up to bat.

Trent had a reputation as a careful pitcher—he just didn't hit batters—and it was only the basketball players who got beaned. When the umpire approached the mound and said, "Son, if you hit one more batter, I'm tossing you out of this game," Trent finally stopped hitting them and started striking them out instead.

When he got back to the dugout, his parents were waiting. Before they could get out a, "What were you thinking?" he began to explain. He told his parents exactly what had happened that night on the basketball court:

"Mom, Dad, you didn't hear what they said and did to Sam. They deserved every single pitch."

To be clear, my point is not, "if someone hurts you or your friend, start honing your fastball." But I'd be lying if I told you my mom didn't relay that story with a smile on her face, and the tightness that had settled in my chest finally released a little. I smiled too. My friend had defended me against those sixth-grade chumps. I wasn't alone. Trent recognized injustice, and even though that wasn't the best way to handle the situation, we all still felt a

51

little proud. It took me awhile to be able to talk to him about it, but early that fall, I simply said, "thank you."

When you have the opportunity to stand up for someone, take it. Find the high road, and a safe and healthy way to handle it, but absolutely take it. When you have the opportunity to support a friend who's being treated badly, do it. Every single time. Although I would encourage you to use your words instead of your arm. Talk to the person being bullied or discriminated against and tell them that you see what's happening. Sometimes just hearing that someone notices and supports you can make all the difference when you are the one who needs to be stood up for. That next fall, when basketball season rolled around again, Trent started playing pretty rough and sent another message pretty early on in the game. Suddenly, every player on that team treated me with total respect and shook my hand after the game.

I wish I could tell you that that was the point I was finally able to get a handle on hurt and anger and how to deal with it properly. Unfortunately, it wasn't. I felt some relief for a moment, but the avalanche that had been building inside of me continued to grow.

What Not to Do with Anger

I could write a book on how not to handle anger, but I'll try and keep it to a few stories so we can talk more about how to use anger for good. What Trent did for me—that felt amazing. He was a good friend and his heart was absolutely in the right place, but what he did was actually quite dangerous. We can laugh about it now, because thankfully, no one was hurt beyond a few bruises, but it could have been catastrophic. He could have seriously hurt someone, which would have only made a bad situation worse. When it comes to anger, I've learned to keep these principles in mind:

1. Never lash out in your anger, physically or verbally; instead practice kindness with both your words and your actions.

Developing the self-control to never physically or verbally cause pain to someone—even if he or she deserves it—is a real test of character. By the time I started seventh grade, the years of teasing, name-calling, and poking fun at my missing hand were really starting to take a toll.

As we all know the bullies in middle school tend to get bigger and meaner. My nemesis that year was a 6'2 skater dude who had it in for me from the first day of school. He and his two sidekicks were the bullies straight from every 90's teen movie and after-school special—pierced grunge dressers with wild mops of hair.

Early in the school year, I got my very first girlfriend. (You know, the kind you call once and awkwardly hold hands with twice?) It took my bully about two seconds to start in on the taunting:

"Are you paying her to go out with you?"
"Gross."
"What girl would go out with him, a guy with one hand? What is wrong with her?"

At this point, my anger lit a long fuse on a stick of dynamite. It was only a matter of time before everything exploded. As one does in the seventh grade, my first girlfriend and I broke up. Our week-long romance was great while it lasted. If only the bullying had stopped after a week too.

For the remainder of the year, Skater Dude and his gauge-pierced sidekicks continued to torment me. And my fuse continued to get shorter and shorter. I never did anything about it. I never said a word to anyone or asked for any kind of help or support. Rather than talking about it with my parents or teachers or anyone who could have stepped in and helped in some way, I stuffed my anger and pain deep inside. Way down deep.

One day in May, as we were all making our way back to our classroom after a break, the topic of girls came up in a conversation with a friend. I slid into my chair and leaned across the aisle to ask my friend his opinion on my current crush:

"So, you really think she might like me? Think she'd go out with me?"

"Yeah," he responded. "I think so. You should ask her."

Unfortunately, Skater Dude was right behind me and heard the whole conversation. Well, there was no way he was going to let a chance to harass me slide, especially with such an easy opening.

"Like you?" he scoffed. "Come on, man. The only way a girl would go out with you is if you paid her."

That was the moment the fuse ran out and the fire of my anger hit the dynamite. Ever heard the phrase "fit of rage?" Yeah, that was me. I grabbed that kid out of his chair so fast and shoved him so hard, I doubt he had any idea what was happening. His buddies joined in, but after nine months of their bullying, they were no match for my temper. I whooped all three of them and sent one of them to the nurse's office.

After the explosion of anger, I looked down at the three bleeding bullies knowing I'd finally shut them up, but it didn't leave me feeling proud. Instead, I felt ashamed. I really hurt them. That wasn't me. That wasn't who I was. And yet, I had done way more damage than I would have ever imagined. As an added bonus, I had three days of in-school suspension to think about what I had done.

I couldn't stand Skater Dude and his minions for what they did to me. They always targeted me when my friends weren't around, and they were so mean and cruel to me that they had slowly chipped away at my confidence. That should have made me never, ever want to cause that kind of pain. But unfortunately, it made me spread it. Like I said, hurt people hurt people. As I looked at what I had done to those kids that day, I also had to face the fact that I'd been bullying other kids too. The kid who didn't smell so great, the smart girl, the kid in the weird clothes. I had been mean to all of them. If I had to be in that pain, I didn't want to have to be in it alone. I hadn't been even close to as mean as Skater Dude had been to me, but I'm sure my words hurt. I was no better than the bullies in the nurse's office. I had hurt people, and I didn't ever want to do that again.

This brings me to my second point. In an effort to not lash out at people—physically or verbally—and to not spread your hurt and anger, do your very best to not let it build up in the first place.

2. Don't stuff your pain or your anger; find strategic ways to release it. Pressure, scientifically, is a measure of force over a specific area.

Pressure is used for all sorts of things. The right amount of pressure can fill up your tires, blow up balloons, or cook a delicious chicken. Too much pressure, and you can explode chicken, latex, and the Michelin Man all over the place.

The same is true for us. It doesn't matter if the pressure comes from others or if you put it on yourself, too much pressure is eventually a recipe for disaster. If we don't take steps to take care of it on the front end, we put ourselves and others at risk when it eventually explodes.

In the moment, it feels like there's nothing we can do. No way to release the anger and the hurt that is piling up inside of us.

The truth is, we can. We probably won't release it or fix it all at once, but we can lessen it slowly, which, over time, can make a big difference.

My teacher that year was a caring woman who had been my babysitter when I was a little boy. After I had to be marched to the principal's office for beating up those three boys, she later caught up with me.

"Sam, I know that what you just did is not who you are. I've been worried about you. I need you to tell me what is going on."

I really needed that grace from her, and I'm so glad she was willing to give it. I just wish I would have talked to her sooner. I told her everything and she encouraged me to be honest with my parents. She spoke to the principal on my behalf and made sure everyone was aware of what had really happened. The boys I beat up ended up with suspensions, too, for their bullying. She also recommended that I spend some time with the school counselor. Talking about the challenges I was facing regularly really helped me.

I learned some important things from this experience. I learned that sometimes, it's okay to have tunnel vision. It's okay to clear out the noise, the bullies, and the naysayers and focus on what matters. Have you ever seen the movie For Love of the Game? It's one of my all-time favorite movies. In it a legendary pitcher named Billy Chapel, played by Kevin Costner, is reliving his baseball career while pitching an away game at Yankee stadium. Yankee fans are notoriously some of the worst hecklers in baseball, and yet, in the midst of that noise, he would say, "clear the mechanism," and suddenly, all he could see was his catcher's glove.

[[callout: Sometimes in life, it's good to zone out and tune out people who are harassing you and focus your vision and your mind on what really matters.]]

Sometimes in life, it's good to zone out and tune out people who are harassing you and focus your vision and your mind on what really matters. We all need to find healthy ways to let go of the negative and zoom our focus in on what matters. Here are some tips on healthy ways to release anger before you get to the point you're about to explode.

How to Handle Anger

Anger is a part of life. It's going to make itself known with our friends, our families, our spouses, our children, and our colleagues. The sooner we can figure out how to handle anger, the better off our lives and relationships will be.

Talk to a safe person. All year long, I had a caring teacher right in front of me, and I never said anything. I never asked for help, and I never brought it to her attention. When we're dealing with any kind of pain, anger, or disappointment, it's so important to find your safe person. A pastor, a teacher, a therapist, a wise friend. Notice I said, "a safe person." I didn't say vent to the whole world or gossip to everyone you know. Find a trustworthy person who lives a life of wisdom and tell them what's going on with you. Sometimes, they might be able to help you solve the issue, but even if they can't "fix" it, it can still do you a world of good to talk it through with them. Healthy conversation over a cup of coffee might not fix your anger or your problem, but it will vent the pressure and help you keep it from building to an unhealthy level.

Take Care of Yourself. Sometimes it's okay to binge watch TV and eat an entire bag of chips to make yourself feel better, but it's not a great long-term plan. The better care we take of ourselves physically, spiritually, and mentally, the better off we will be. Feel like you're getting to the boiling point? Think about some of these things:

Are you tired? Getting enough sleep is key to so many parts of life, especially dealing with our anger. Take a nap. Seriously. It helps.

How's your diet? Food does all kinds of crazy things to our bodies, and subsisting on junk food, fast food, and sugar—though it all is so delicious in the moment—isn't doing anything to promote our physical or mental health. Some foods can actually worsen anxiety. So think about what you're eating. Also, drink more water. It can be easier than you think to become a little dehydrated. It's easier to deal with difficult things when your body and brain have the nutrition they need.

Do you need to go for a walk? A walk, a run, a bike ride. Whatever, just get moving. Exercise can help release the pressure valve in a very positive way. Find something you enjoy doing and reap the benefits of getting healthier and dealing with anger and frustration. (As I said earlier, I definitely took some frustration out with fastballs and the side of a shed over the years.)

Read, meditate, and pray. When I need wisdom, I read the Bible, pray, and try to focus my mind on God's Word—not the thing I'm mad about. This is a real act of the will. Sometimes I don't do it. Sometimes I get mad and stay mad for too long before I turn to God. But who is that really helping? Here are some great verses to meditate on:

He who is slow to anger is better than the mighty,
And he who rules his spirit than he who takes a city.

Proverbs 16:32 nkjv

And "don't sin by letting anger control you." Don't let the sun go down while you are still angry, for anger gives a foothold to the devil.

Ephesians 4:26–27 nlt

Don't sin by letting anger control you.
  Think about it overnight and remain silent.

Psalm 4:4 nlt

Finally, brothers and sisters, whatever is true, whatever is noble,
whatever is right, whatever is pure, whatever is lovely, whatever is
admirable—if anything is excellent or praiseworthy—think about
such things.

Philippians 4:8 niv

Think about the future. My sophomore year of high school, I almost made an epic mistake. The coach who would later tell me I would never make it in college had promised me that I would pitch in a game, and then at the last minute started someone else. I was so mad. He'd hardly let me pitch all year—only three games against teams he thought for sure would beat us—and I won every single time. And, it wasn't just me who struggled under his coaching. He intimidated a lot of my teammates. My personal injustice as I saw it, was just one of many my teammates were also enduring. The quiet boys. The nice ones. Those of us who respected authority and weren't big on bucking the rules. My dad never said anything to a coach about playing time. He told me he never would. That would always be my problem to solve. But, my dad began watching the coach closely, noting the comments, promises, and degrading remarks. I walked by the coach as the starting pitcher threw out the first ball and said, "You lied." I walked out of the dugout near tears. He came out after with his chest pushed out and shoulders back— just like someone does when they want to fight. We got into a shouting match, and when he got in my face. Well, it was about to get ugly. Real ugly. I was about to blow again.

"Hold up!" My dad's voice rang in my ears, and he jumped in between me and the coach. My dad calmed everyone down and diffused the situation like a pro. Thank God he did that. I was so mad at that coach, but looking back I know I would have been in huge trouble if my dad hadn't intervened. And not only that, I would have let my anger destroy my future and the one goal I had been working so hard at for so long. It's one thing for a university baseball program to take a chance on a kid with one hand, it's another if he's also a kid with a reputation for hitting coaches. My dad reminded me later that you have to pick your battles carefully, especially with someone who wields authority over you. Reacting in anger usually doesn't get you what you want and it almost always makes the situation worse, no matter how justified that anger may be.

Think about your future. Don't let your anger screw it up.

I've learned these things over the years as I navigated pain and anger over the way others treated me because of my limb difference. I messed up a lot, but I also picked up some things along the way. I was a little older before I realized that if managed properly, anger could actually be a great thing.

Use Your Anger for Good

This might sound strange, but anger can be good and necessary. The ultimate key here is learning what to do about it and how to use your anger for good. You can spend about 15 seconds on Facebook and realize just how angry the world is. Everyone is mad about something, and no one seems to be handling it very well. And, honestly, most of the time we're not even angry about the right things!

If you think about game changers throughout history, they had some real, urgent things to be mad about and they put all of their anger and energy toward making the world better.

Dr. Martin Luther King, Jr. was pretty upset about segregation and the way black people were treated in America. Just like Nelson Mandela was angry about the lack of justice and human equality during apartheid in South Africa. Young David was righteously offended that Goliath would speak against Israel and said in 1 Samuel 17, "For who is this uncircumcised Philistine, that he should defy the armies of the living God?" (v. 26, nkjv).

And then the young shepherd boy faced his giant and said, "You come to me with a sword, with a spear, and with a javelin. But I come to you in the name of the Lord of hosts, the God of the armies of Israel, whom you have defied. This day the Lord will deliver you into my hand" (vv. 45–46, nkjv).

I think he was mad. I think David was furious that someone was going to war against his people and talking trash about his God. And rightly so. He used that anger as fuel and to help him focus on trusting God when he walked out on the battlefield against Goliath. He was a young boy, but he bravely stepped out as a warrior in defense of God and his people.

Even Jesus was angry.

The Passover of the Jews was near, and Jesus went up to Jerusalem. In the temple he found people selling cattle, sheep, and doves, and the money changers seated at their tables. Making a whip of cords, he drove all of them out of the temple, both the sheep and the cattle. He also poured out the coins of the money changers and overturned their tables. He told those who were selling the doves, "Take these things out of here! Stop making my Father's house a marketplace!" His disciples remembered that it was written, "Zeal for your house will consume me." —John 2:13–17 NRSV

This passage always reminds me that anger is not actually a sin and that God wants us to be consumed, angry, and passionate about some things. You see, when God gets angry, it's a holy anger. So often when we get angry, it's fueled from selfishness—it's anger about our hurts, our disappointments, and about our unmet expectations. That's a lot different than being angry on behalf of others, on behalf of a righteous God. He wants us to be full of compassion, angered by injustice, and brave enough to funnel all of that toward doing good for His glory.

I could have stayed mad about how people treated me. I could have kept sending kids to the nurse's office and making cutting remarks to other kids who hadn't ever done anything to me because I was so full of anger and pain. Instead, I decided I didn't want to be that guy. Bullies are jerks. Why would I want to be a jerk?

Once I chose to use anger for good and turn away from that bullying behavior, incredible things began to happen. I was able to meet people I might have overlooked otherwise and form amazing relationships. I had some more hurdles to overcome, but God was about to set me on my path and start opening my eyes to my purpose.

Anger can be a path toward destruction or a bridge toward incredible good. Neither path is easy, but only one is worth the trouble.

Chapter 6
Eliminate Your Fear of Failure

What Amazing Things Would We Do If We Were Free And Unafraid?

"Everything you want is on the other side of fear."

Jack Canfield

The flames flickered and danced against the summer night sky as I stood around the campfire with strangers who would later become friends. Friends who would change my life forever. The campfire lit up the smiling faces of other teenagers and children with limb differences. At some point in my sixteen years, one would have thought I would have met other kids like me, but I hadn't.

We were going around the circle taking turns introducing ourselves and sharing about the sports we played and hobbies we liked. I was with other teen counselors like myself, younger kids who were campers, and a whole lot of parents.

"Hi, I'm Jeff. I'm from Michigan. I'm missing my right hand, and I play soccer."

"Hey, I'm Stef. I was born without part of my left arm. I love playing soccer."

"Soccer." "Soccer." "Soccer."

Every kid played soccer. Like, every single one. Nothing against soccer. Truly. Although, in small Midwestern towns where people eat, sleep, and drink American football, we don't tend to see a whole lot of soccer. I couldn't help but curl my lip, and think: Soccer? Really? Plus, they all had two feet, so what was hard about that?

So when it was my turn to introduce myself, I chimed in, "Hey, I'm Sam. I was born without my left hand, but I'm a baseball pitcher, a center on the basketball team, and a tight end on the football team." I might have gotten a little carried away; I didn't really want to be the kind of guy who brags, but I also wanted to make sure people realized that just because we're limb-different doesn't mean we have to be limited in the sports we play and opportunities we chase after. Just because we don't have two hands doesn't mean we have to exclusively play sports that primarily use our feet.

I might have taken it a step too far, because then I may or may not have made a remark about the you have two-feet/how fun can that be? Situation . . . and then I said soccer was a sin where I came from.

My mother may or may not have elbowed me hard in the ribs.

I wasn't trying to be mean. I was seriously perplexed as to why that was the only sport they had ever played. As the evening wore on, I started to figure it out.

They were afraid of failure—or, and this was the bigger issue—their parents were afraid of their failure. These kids had never even had an opportunity to try anything else. Their parents knew they could succeed in soccer because hands weren't necessary in that sport. Suddenly, I was incredibly grateful for parents who threw me into the pool because they knew I could swim. Who took off my training wheels and told me to go for it. Who signed me up for baseball and basketball and football and let me take a chance.

You can't learn how to really win if you've never lost.

[[callout: You can't learn how to really win if you've never lost.]]

As soon as I got this figured out, I pulled my mom aside.

"Hey, do you think you could get these parents out of here for a little bit? These kids, I think they want a chance to play, to try new things. And everyone keeps trying to talk to me about soccer," I said with a hint of disdain.

She understood immediately, and suddenly, the campers' moms and dads were happily having an informal mentoring session with my mom. While my mom was sharing about what it was like to parent a limb-different teenage athlete, the other counselors and I headed to the gym with our campers, and we got to work. Within 45 minutes, these kids were making catches and doing glove transfers with baseballs; they were dribbling basketballs like they'd been doing it for ages. They were amazing. They had so much raw talent and were so quickly picking up skills that I'd spent years trying to hone.

I was in awe. I was sad. I was full of joy. All at once. How do you help people who are too afraid to try? How do you help children who have parents who are too afraid to let them try new things?

I wasn't exactly sure, but I knew I was going to do my best to figure it out.

At one point, early in the camp but after our introductions, another counselor came up to me. "You said you play football, right? Let me throw you some passes." And then this kid, who was missing his arms from his elbows down began to throw me the most incredible spiral passes. My jaw dropped in disbelief. These kids were amazing.

Later, my mom found me in my room in our cabin, alone, with my face in my hands and tears pouring down my face. "Sam, what's wrong?" She sat down next to me, and I lifted my head and looked at her with the biggest smile on my face.

"This is the greatest thing that has ever happened to me," I said. "I will never feel sorry for myself about this another day in my life." And I hugged her and kept crying.

That camp changed me in three ways:

It healed me from my past.
It prepared me for my future.
It helped me let go of my fear of failure.

By that time in my life, I had come a long way dealing with the questions, hurt, and anger about my limb difference. But being with these kids and other teenagers like me was what finally set me free. It was like God placed me in the most perfect spot to see the full spectrum of people I needed in my life—from those who were like me and could help me finally accept myself to others who were also like me but needed help from me. I've heard that you should always have older, wiser people as mentors in your life, and likewise, you should always be mentoring younger people who need you. I needed to be completely healed from my past, so I could move on to my future and be able to help others.

[[callout: "This is the greatest thing that has ever happened to me. I will never feel sorry for myself about this another day in my life."]]

That camp changed my life in so many ways. It opened my eyes to some realities about failure, and it created a passion in me to help others let go of their fears of failure. As it turns out, I think we give failure too much power to negatively affect us, and we don't think about the power failure has for good. That's right. There is a lot of positive power in failing.

3 Ways Failure Can Be Awesome

These kids and their parents opened my eyes to the reality of what it's like to live in fear of failure. Fear is awful. It's the worst. But failure? It's actually not so bad. Think about this with me for a second:

Failure teaches us. Thomas Edison said, "I have not failed. I've just found 10,000 ways that didn't work." Can you imagine the wealth of information and things he must have learned from those 10,000 ways that didn't work—those 10,000 failures, if you will? I bet he became more and more of an expert with his materials and his craft every single time he failed. That's the key right there. We have to pay attention. We have to learn. Then every single time something doesn't work or we fail in some way, we can go on to try again and be smarter and stronger than we were before. Failure is an excellent teacher; we just have to pay attention. What would have happened if Thomas Edison had quit or given up 1,000 times into his experiment? I'd be writing this book with an ink pen by the glowing light of a candle. I think we could argue that if we learned something that equips us for the future, it probably can't even be classified as a failure.

Believe it or not, failure—and learning from failure—is one of the reasons why I love sports. Many sports, like my favorite, baseball, are games of failure. Hitting the ball every time you come up to the plate in a game is basically impossible. Throwing strikes every single pitch without them getting launched is something not even the greatest pitchers of all time could accomplish. Getting thrown out, gunned down, dropping the ball—failure is just part of the game. When you strike out, when you drop the pass, when you miss the spike—these are failures that every athlete experiences. Those failures teach us to grind more, play smarter, and increase our desire to win. But you have to be willing to learn. You have to have the confidence to take each failure, learn from it, practice what you've learned, and let that failure push you to succeed the next time, so you can be the one who is saying "Hit it to me!" or "Go ahead and swing on me!" You have to be the one who is confident because of your past failures that you know how to win. Sports are a safe place to fail. I think we all should see that. Even if we don't actually like failing.

Failure makes us kinder and more empathetic. Sometimes failure and hardship bring healthy humility and perspective to our lives. Failure's rough blow to our pride can also soften our hearts. When you've failed, it can light a fire in you for others facing the same type of failure. Instead of looking to others with judgment, we can look to them with understanding and empathy. A few good failures make us better, wiser, kinder people.

Failure both closes and opens doors. Can I tell you about a few times I'm so glad I failed?

What if I hadn't gotten cut from baseball in middle school? I might not have practiced and tried so hard. I might have made teams but never moved ahead or achieved my college goals.

What if that cute blonde hadn't rejected me? Well, I might not be marrying the prettiest brunette I've ever seen.

We so easily lose sight of the fact that we all have very limited perspectives. Even the most brilliant people on earth are not all-knowing. We don't have the whole picture, and we don't have a clear picture. The Bible tells us, "For now we see in a mirror dimly, but then face to face. Now I know in part; then I shall know fully, even as I have been fully known" (1 Cor. 13:12, esv.) We're human, and we can only see part of the picture.

In the moment, failure might seem like the worst thing that could have happened to us. But what if that failure closed a door to a path that would have been terrible for you? Or what if it closed a door that then allowed another to open? In this life, we won't have all the answers. But we can commit ourselves and our choices to a

God who is bigger, wiser, and who knows all. He has a clear view of the whole picture, and we can trust Him.

What do you think would happen if we let go of our fear of failure? Bestselling author of the Chicken Soup series and motivational speaker Jack Canfield asked, "What if everything you want is on the other side of fear?"

Think about that for a second. What if everything you want is on the other side of fear?

First, we have to think about everything we want. What is it that you really, really want? Think of everything from trivial wants to serious, meaningful desires. Is it a better relationship with someone? A spouse, a new job, friends? A healthier body or more time for yourself? More time with your family?

Second, think about all the things that are holding you back. Why don't you have those things that you want? What would you have to do to get them?

And finally, what are you afraid of? What is really holding you back? Let's look at a few people who faced epic fears, and then let's walk ourselves all the way through our own so we can identify both what it is we really long for and the things that are standing in our way.

Some fears are really hard. Life is full of things we can't control: accidents, natural disasters, illnesses, the actions and behaviors of other people. God tells us in numerous places in the Bible to fear not; I think we can take comfort that that command is for things we have absolutely no control over as well as the things we might actually have a little bit of influence on. Every game changer I've ever met at some point had to stare his or her fears in the face and then let them go. Some of them had to beat them with a stick. Others had to climb mountains to get past them. But one way or the other, each of them had to eliminate their fears so they could move forward.

Shaquem Griffin was drafted by the Seattle Seahawks to play in the NFL in 2018. He has a nub like mine. He, too, was always told he wouldn't be able to compete at the next level. He almost listened to the doubters and quit. But he didn't. He didn't let fear stop him. His story parallels mine in many ways. Except, of course, the part where he made it to the pros.

My friend Jarred Bullock was a green beret. He lost both his arm just below his shoulder and his leg just below the knee in Afghanistan. He also lost his friends and comrades to the right and left of him. He could have quit. Instead, he mustered up every bit of will power he had to embrace the opportunity, face the fear of his new body, and compete against people with two hands and feet less than a year after his injuries in tough mudder competitions.

In the Bible, Queen Esther was faced with an epic dilemma. Her people were about to be victims of genocide if she didn't intervene. However, if she did intervene on their behalf, she, too, could have faced death. Even though she was married to the king, she was still not allowed to approach him unless summoned, as she told her cousin Mordecai: "All the king's servants and the people of the king's provinces know that if any man or woman goes to the king inside the inner court without being called, there is but one law—to be put to death, except the one to whom the king holds out the golden scepter so that he may live. But as for me, I have not been called to come in to the king these thirty days." (Est 4:11, esv).

And Mordecai responded in verse 14, "For if you keep silent at this time, relief and deliverance will rise for the Jews from another place, but you and your father's house will perish. And who knows whether you have not come to the kingdom for such a time as this?"

Think about that last sentence for just a minute and think about it for your own life. And who knows whether you have not come to the kingdom for such a time as this? Apply that to your current situation, your current fears and dreams: Who knows if you're here right now for such a time as this?

So what did Esther do? She overcame her fear and said in verse 16: "Then I will go to the king, though it is against the law, and if I perish, I perish."

Wow. Most of us aren't up against that kind of fear, that kind of pressure, to save an entire people. Even in the face of that, Esther chose courage over fear, bravery in the face of the fiercest opposition. And when Esther stood before the King, he reached out to her with his golden scepter.

Not only did the king welcome Esther to speak with him instead of sending her to her death, he told her she may ask whatever she wished, and it would be given to her, up to half of his kingdom. She requested he and Haman—the instigator of the genocide—let her prepare two banquets for them. In Esther 7:2–6 (nlt), the king queries his queen:

On this second occasion, while they were drinking wine, the king again said to Esther, "Tell me what you want, Queen Esther. What is your request? I will give it to you, even if it is half the kingdom!"

Queen Esther replied, "If I have found favor with the king, and if it pleases the king to grant my request, I ask that my life and the lives of my people will be spared. For my people and I have been sold to those who would kill, slaughter, and annihilate us. If we had merely been sold as slaves, I could remain quiet, for that would be too trivial a matter to warrant disturbing the king."

"Who would do such a thing?" King Xerxes demanded. "Who would be so presumptuous as to touch you?"

Esther replied, "This wicked Haman is our adversary and our enemy." Haman grew pale with fright before the king and queen.

Spoiler alert. Things didn't go well for Haman. The king left the room in a rage; while he was gone, Haman fell upon Esther's couch to beg for mercy just when the king re-entered the room. The scene did not look good, and the king was even more furious as it looked like he was now assaulting the queen. Haman was executed that very day. Today, the Jewish people still celebrate Purim, a holiday that commemorates the Jews being saved from Haman.

Think about your fear again. That big I can't do it because what if _____ happens? The one that's holding you back from taking a big step toward your dream. Now, think about the worst thing that can happen if you try? Walk yourself all the way through it. I know there are missionaries and Christians all over the world who are facing life and death opposition like Esther. You might be wrestling with something on that level. But a lot of us let other types of fear overwhelm us. Fears that don't necessarily involve life and death consequences. That doesn't mean that overcoming that fear doesn't matter, that it isn't important. Walk yourself all the way through your fears and the worst-case scenario:

Does the girl turn you down and break your heart forever? Did you miss out on the dream job? Are you back to ground zero? Did you find out you really don't love living in that city after all? Do you fall flat on your face after you've tried the thing that you love, the thing that you really, desperately want to do? At the end of it, now ask yourself this:

Is God still God?
Do I believe He is in control?
Is my first goal to serve Him well and help others?
Do I trust Him?

[[callout: Have I not commanded you? Be strong and courageous. Do not be afraid; do not be discouraged, for the Lord your God will be with you wherever you go." —Joshua 1:9 niv]]

I can't tell you the exact answer to your question. But I can tell you with certainty that fear is not from God, and I can promise you that He will be with you wherever you go. Don't make hasty decisions, ask for His guidance, and trust Him.

[[callout: For God has not given us a spirit of fear, but of power and of love and of a sound mind. —2 Timothy 1:7 nkjv]]

Remember what we learned about failure? Even if you go the worst no of your life or you actually did fall flat on your face, you're probably not at ground zero. Odds are, you learned something that will equip you for next time. If you walked into it with an open heart, you're probably a better, nicer person. And who knows what doors might open from those steps you took, the people you met, and the connections you made?

Now, ask this yourself the question again, and take it to the best-case scenario? What if you do achieve your dream? What if you make it? What if the King holds out his golden scepter to you? What if everything you're dreaming of is on the other side of your fear?

Several years ago, a teenage boy who was missing his right hand showed up at our NubAbility camp. Now, most of our camp kids who come are typically under the age of 12, and Kevin was 16 at the time. I'm guessing that made him more than a little uncomfortable, but he came anyway.

When he got to us, he had been cut from his freshman and sophomore baseball teams. I have to tell you; it's really hard to come back from that. When you're in high school, and you weren't able to make the junior varsity teams, it's exceptionally hard to make varsity. But Kevin wasn't going to let his fear get in the way of his dreams. Even if it meant asking for help. Even if it was super uncomfortable. Even if he was afraid.

Kevin showed up and worked hard, and can I tell you what was on the other side of his fear? College baseball. Now he's a pitcher for a university, and he's living out his dream.

73

What if you woke up tomorrow and fear had been completely eliminated from your life? Imagine, stretching under the covers, seeing the sunlight filtering through your curtains, and feeling the weightless absence of fear. It's glorious. You take a deep breath, smile, and don't feel even an ounce of tension in your shoulders. You feel great. You feel confident. You feel ready to take on your day—and you're looking ahead at it with anticipation. Not dread.

You. Can. Do. This. I promise you. You can let your fear of failure go.

We have to let it go if we want to be able to live lives of impact. It's like hauling around a sack of bricks. And once you drop it, you'll be amazed.

That night I was talking about before? That night I took all those soccer-loving kids into the gym at camp and let them try other sports. It was astounding. Kids who had never touched a basketball—who were so afraid of how they might look or what people might say—were laughing, having a great time, and learning new skills. Some of them were incredibly talented! And if they hadn't ever tried, they would have missed out on so much. I remembered how I used to have their struggle, how I was so afraid that I'd mess up and never be allowed back on the mound again. I knew I needed to do something bigger for these kids and all the kids out there like them.

I got into the car after those three days at camp and looked at my mom. "Mom," I said with conviction, "those kids were so afraid and they were missing out on so many good things. I want to do something to change it. I want to help them." I then went on to describe the vision I had for what would later become Nubability:

"I want a sports camp for limb-different kids, and I want it coached by limb-different athletes like me. I want to help them to let go of their fears. And to help their parents let go of their fears. These kids need a chance. I think if I had a few days with them, I could really help them realize what they are capable of doing."

My mom listened to every word I said, and she took me very seriously. This was a pretty big deal in light of the fact that I was her goofball, jock of a son who only ever got Cs. Not because I wasn't smart enough to get better grades, but because I was too busy working on sports to work on school. I put in a minimal amount of effort to get Cs because my dad wouldn't let me play if I got Ds. But like always, my mom believed in me.

"Son," she said, "I'd have driven you across the country on my last ten dollar bill if I'd known how much this would help you and help others. Of course I will help you start your camp."

She wasn't afraid that we'd fail, and she let me take a chance. Again. Like always. My mom made a pact with me on that drive home. She promised she'd help me figure out how to create a non-profit and start a sports camp to help these kids and their parents. Together, we were going to find a way to do this.

Those few days with those campers changed my life. I was going to help these kids and others like them. I was going to tell them how I wrote Philippians 4:13 (nkjv) all over every piece of sports equipment I owned. I was going to tell them how repeating "I can do all things through Christ who strengthens me" over and over again helped me actually believe it. I was going to teach them how hard work can pay off, how using anger for good things can change their lives, and how if they can just let go of the fear of failure, amazing things could be waiting for them. One way or another, it was going to happen. I was going to help.

God was about to open a door for me that would change my life and the lives of others. I almost missed it, but then something happened that gave me no choice but to wake up and pay attention.

Chapter 7
Let Go of Your Pride and Embrace Your Redemption

It's The Greatest Trade You'll Ever Make

"Grace is God as a heart surgeon, cracking open your chest, removing your heart— poisoned as it is with pride and pain—and replacing it with his own."

Max Lucado

Pride is a funny thing. It's one of those sins that creep up over time. It's like the frog in the pot of water. One second you're just swimming in a hot tub, enjoying the warmth, and the next, the water's hit the boiling point and you're really getting burned.

By the time my senior year of high school rolled around, I was feeling much better about things. Baseball was going pretty well and some colleges started calling. I had finally started letting go of my anger and insecurities. Unfortunately, I started replacing those things with pride.

I got a call from a college baseball team during the fall of my senior year. They scheduled a time for me to come and tour the campus. I was beyond thrilled. Finally. I was finally getting my chance.

"Look at that field, Sam. Next year you could be pitching out there." The assistant coach showed me the entire campus and the baseball field. I loved every bit of it. I was so ready and so pumped. And then we got to the head coach's office.

He was a great guy; he really was. But somehow, before he said a word I felt like I was about to be in trouble or get bad news. He sat me down that day and said, "Son, you're the type of leader we look for; I'm just not sure if you're going to be able to compete. We'll keep watching."

All I could think was, why on earth would you bring me here just to tell me that? But I decided I wasn't going to get down like I used to. I knew I was good enough to compete. I was one of the top players on our Varsity team, dang it! I was going to prove to them and everyone else that I could do it. If it had been all drive, work ethic, and ambition propelling me forward, that probably would have been okay. But this time it was an unhealthy pride that was compelling me, and a whole lot of it.

I decided I would spend the whole year focusing on baseball, so I gave up basketball my senior year. That was a terrible idea. Instead of giving me time to focus on baseball, it took away the structure and discipline of being an athlete on a varsity sport. What it really gave me more time for was partying. I started having a lot of fun with the wrong people. That didn't help my fastball or my character.

Life was good, but I wasn't. I felt pretty good, and I was having fun. But I wasn't living how I should have been living. I decided I was a Christian who didn't need to go to church. Spring came around, and my pride and my head kept growing. My fastball was faster, and it was right on point. I could hit a can from 60 feet away. That college called back, and this time they signed me. I had finally done it. I was going to be a college baseball pitcher. I should have been grateful for all God had done and all He had blessed me with, but instead, I convinced myself that it was my hard work that got me that scholarship and that place on the team. I thought I was responsible for my good fortune.

I graduated from high school feeling good about myself and decided I was going to have an exceptionally great summer. There's an unspoken rule that you don't play ball the summer after high school. So again, instead of playing a sport, I started partying hard every single weekend and doing all sorts of things I had no business doing.

I was living how I wanted to be living and doing what I wanted to be doing. I was putting myself first, and I wasn't serving God or anyone else. Some people live like this for decades—the whole of their lives. I can see how it would be easy to do that. There's a reason it's called temptation—the sin I was dabbling in was tempting. It felt good, at least in the short term.

But I got a wake-up call my freshman year of college that changed my life forever.

My first year of college started well. I thought I was ready to turn over a new leaf and leave behind some of the bad habits I'd started picking up. I started going to chapel and trying to make better choices. Unfortunately, that only lasted for a couple weeks, and then my pride started changing my direction again. I wanted to be liked and accepted and my new friends at college liked me and treated me just like anyone else so long as I was partying with them. Rocking the boat and saying no meant standing out, and I really, really wanted to be accepted, to feel cool and popular, especially after all the bullying I'd gone through in middle and high school. I didn't want to feel like an outsider, and my pride in my status as a college athlete made me feel like I deserved to be popular and let loose at a few different parties each weekend. At least I had the discipline of a sport again, so I had a little less time for trouble.

College baseball workouts were intense. Extremely intense. Being a college pitcher is code for also being a runner. On the first day of practice, Coach looked at me and the other P.O. (pitcher only) and said, "Alright boys. Five miles. Get going."

All I could think was, oh, crap . . .

Some guys quit over that run, but I sure wasn't quitting now. I didn't quit during hell week's two-a-day practices, and I showed up for weights and cardio every day at 5:00 a.m. I submitted myself to the discipline of college baseball, and it was working for me. My fastball was getting more awesome by the day, and I was in the best shape of my life. If my priorities off the field had been in order, things could have been good.

That October, I got a text from my grandfather: "Hey Boy, Cardinals are in the World Series. Want to go?"

We were lifelong cardinals fans. Of course I wanted to go! Some fast googling showed that the games were, of course, sold out.

"Granddaddy, tickets are sold out."

"Boy, don't you worry. Your granddaddy's got connections."

And just like that, I found myself five rows back from the visiting dugout with my granddaddy and my brothers. It was one of the most amazing nights of my life. St. Louis is one of the greatest baseball towns in America, and the game ended up being historic. Unreal does not begin to describe it.

This was game six of the Rangers/Cards series in 2011. If you know baseball, you know that that game went down in history. The Cards came from behind and forced extra innings. The stadium looked like a sea of rally towels, and more than 45,000 people were on their feet. David Freese, a kid who grew up in the suburbs of St. Louis stepped up to the plate and hit a home run in the eleventh inning to win the game.

It was awesome.

David Freese became the ultimate hometown hero, and the camaraderie and celebration of the 45,000 people in that stadium exploded into the October sky. It was definitely one of the greatest nights of my life

The next morning, I got up early and made my way to practice for one of our final workouts of the year. That night, my buddies and I sat around the student lounge to watch Game 7, the game David Freese's masterful homerun had forced. By the sixth inning, we couldn't stand. We had to get to St. Louis, and we knew we could get there before it was over.

The city was electric. We got to Busch Stadium and were actually able to stand outside the left field fence and see the game. It was so crowded, but that's definitely one of the perks of being 6'5". The only thing that could possibly top a historic comeback in Game 6 is a win for Game 7.

"Cards win! Cards win!"

It was apocalyptic madness. I've never seen anything like it before or since. The city erupted in celebration, and the streets became a party—an epic, crazy party. It took us almost four hours to make a 45-minute drive; I've never seen so many fender benders where, rather than being mad, strangers were getting out of their cars, fist-bumping, high-fiving and shouting, "Dude, Cards won!" I'll bet the insurance companies were thrilled.

We ate greasy sliders in the middle of the night and collapsed in our dorm beds. My roommate that year was a catcher. He liked the temperature a lot warmer than I did, so we'd wrestle for control of the thermostat. I was a lot bigger than he was . . . that night he put a hoodie on without saying a word and made the room cooler. Even with the cool room, and the window by my bed open, I remember going to sleep feeling pretty warm.

I woke the next morning, a Sunday, and went to morning devotions. I'd planned to go workout, but I was so tired that I went back to my dorm room to take a nap. I woke up a little bit later in the day feeling terrible. Absolutely awful. I had never felt that sick in my entire life. I was so dizzy I couldn't see straight, and I could hardly move. My head was spinning and I fell down twice on my way to the bathroom to throw up. My mom called me several times to see how the night went and to check in with me. I was sick and oblivious. I never answered.

Later in the day, my mom checked in with my roommate to see how I was doing since I hadn't answered her calls all day. "Not so great," was his reply. "He says he has chills, and he's shaking pretty violently." She asked him to take my temperature and it showed 103. She got in the car and came to get me. When she found me, I was burning up with a fever and drenched in sweat, but I still felt like I was freezing.

If you have to be sick, the best place to be is home. My mom started filling me with sports drinks before we ever left campus. When we got home later that night, I went straight to the basement. The man cave. For some reason, that was always the spot for sick people at our house. It was cool and comfortable, and I crashed hard on the couch.

I started feeling a little better the next day and was certain I'd be back in class by Wednesday. I went upstairs and sent notes to my professors that Monday morning and continued to recuperate on the couch. Then, in a matter of hours, everything changed.

When I woke up the next day, I couldn't even move. I was burning up with a fever again and was barely coherent. My mom tried everything to get me upstairs to get me to the hospital, but I just couldn't do it. She had to call my dad back from work. I was 6'5" and 225 pounds, and my father had to carry me up the stairs and out to the car. My parents took me straight to the hospital in

Carbondale. My small town has a hospital, but we all went to Carbondale for anything that seemed serious.

I don't remember a thing about that drive, but I'm told my dad was pushing around a hundred miles per hour. When I got to the emergency room, the doctors and nurses hooked me up to IVs and started running tests immediately. Blood tests, IVs, CT scans. They did not waste any time. My liver and spleen were dangerously enlarged, and I was admitted to stay overnight. Nausea settled back in, and I became overcome with the most violent shakes I've ever had. To this day, I've never seen or even heard of something like this, but my body began to shake so violently, it was like someone had a hold of my shoulders and was shaking the life out of me. This went on for days. By day seven, I was reciting the Lord's Prayer over and over and over again. The Lord's Prayer had always brought me comfort, and I was desperate for comfort and desperate for the shakes to subside.

The doctors were puzzled by the results that started coming in. They were indicative of some type of tick-born illness like Rocky Mountain spotted fever, but they were not conclusive. They began to load my system with heavy antibiotics and IV meds to try to control my fever while they continued to run tests.

Our pastor and a friend from church came to see me, and they picked up on the concern from the doctors and nurses right away. They reached out to our congregation and got people praying immediately. My mom reached out on social media, and before we knew it, people from all over the world were praying for me.

The medicines did not work on my fever. I mean, I guess they could have kept it at 104.6 instead of 105, but nothing would get it lower than that. For the next four days, the infectious disease doctor at the hospital was testing me for everything under the sun. Meanwhile, my liver began to fail, and my normally pinkish skin turned the color of Dijon mustard. My parents told me later that they could see the swollen lymph nodes sticking out all over my body from across the room. My lymph nodes were swelling in places I didn't even know I had lymph nodes.

On day five, the infectious disease doctor literally packed me on ice. She pulled all my medication because my liver was failing, put me on a new antibiotic, and ordered I be packed in ice bags to see if that would break my 103–105 degree temperature streak. During those five days, my parents never left my side. They prayed continually. My brothers, coaches, and teammates cycled in and out of my room, though, I can't say I remember a whole lot of detail.

My parents began to advocate that I be moved to a larger hospital. Our infectious disease doctor had stayed in touch with colleagues in St. Louis, and she came in and said, "Son, we're going to take you in for some lymph node biopsies while we wait for a bed to open up in the liver unit at the hospital in St. Louis."

They did the biopsy, my condition continued to deteriorate, and an ambulance was brought to take me to St. Louis University hospital. My parents had tried desperately to get me in to see a highly successful liver doctor there who was known for healing many people—including famous people—of their liver ailments. It was a long shot, but my doctor got us the referral. A week after my mother had driven to Greenville to pick me up from college, we found ourselves in an ambulance on our way to St. Louis. The hospital gave my mother a stack of my medical records that was three inches thick.

When we arrived, the liver specialist who'd taken my case was flown out to another city to perform an emergency liver transplant. We were also assigned an infectious disease doctor. He was a cheerful, grandiose sort of man, and he'd been the only doctor my parents had spoken with who exhibited any sort of confidence. "It's mono, mono, MONO!" He'd say in his booming voice.

"Did he test positive for that?" My parents would ask.

"Nope, not yet. But I'm testing him again."

"How," my mother asked, "Can Sam be this sick and it be mono?"

"Mono kills kids every day," he said matter-of-factly.

Well, that was less than reassuring. My fourth mono test came back negative.

I have to tell you, of all the times in life you want to be a standout, a rock star, or a complete original—being in the hospital is not one of those times. No one could figure out what was wrong with me, and I had doctor after doctor emerging seemingly from the woodwork to poke and prod me. Everyone was intrigued by my mystery illness. I think even the maintenance men stopped by to get a look. And although St. Louis was a bigger, better hospital, my feet hung off the edge of their small hospital beds too.

On my third day in St. Louis, my mom got a call from the infectious disease doctor in Carbondale. She said very sternly to my mother: "A doctor is going to come into Sam's room and give you a piece of paper. It is going to have a pathology report and a probable diagnosis on it from the lymph node biopsies the ENT took on Saturday. This report is scary. I don't want you to believe it yet. You need to dig in your heels and do not waiver until every director of every department at St. Louis University Hospital has seen your boy. The pathology results show on the report as Acute Multi-Lymphatic Castleman's Disease. It's not cancer, it's worse. There is no treatment and the life expectancy was a few weeks to a few months."

My mother hit her knees, and my father quickly held her and ushered her to the waiting room. I only know through the story what happened next.

My mother tried to explain through her sobs to my father what she'd just been told when a young resident approached them with a sheet of paper and a message no person ever wants to receive. Hearing the words out loud again and reading them in black and white made it so much worse. When you're as sick as I was, you end up in pretty sad parts of hospitals. In that waiting room, my parents were oblivious to everything else going on around them. Oblivious to the family sitting there while their dad was dying. Oblivious to the son of the mom who needed a liver transplant soon or she would never see him play college baseball. Oblivious to the young resident in the white coat who decided right then and there that he was going into orthopedics. The only thing they were aware of was the searing, gut-wrenching pain. My mama's spirit was broken in that moment. She cried out for God . . . and that's when she saw Him.

She saw Him in my father when he took her face in his hands and through his tears said, "We can do this. Families do this every day. I pray this is not the diagnosis, but if it is we can get through this. And," he continued on to say, "this just may not be about us. It may not be about Sam. Maybe this is about something much bigger than us."

My parents came into my room and huddled together with me over my bed. I knew something was very wrong by the looks on their faces. They told me the truth of what they heard, and then they immediately began to pray. My mother, who moments before was near collapse, was now praying over me confidently and boldly. She told God how thankful they were to be my parents, she prayed for my healing in Jesus' Name, she promised if I were healed we would help children like me all over the world, and then she laid me down at His throne.

We were terrified, but together, we were going to fight. And we remembered that perhaps this wasn't about us.

I thought I had been poked and prodded before, well this news opened the floodgates. Nationally known directors of the hospital were practically waiting in line outside my room. More scans. More tests. And we were blessed with another infectious disease doctor who ordered more lymph node biopsies.

I continued to get weaker, more yellow, and my liver numbers continued to plummet. In the midst of this, my amazing parents carried on, trying as much as they could to remember that maybe this wasn't all about us. My dad shared an elevator with a man who lost his son in an accident and wasn't sure if his wife was going to make it. No words exist to bring comfort to something like that. My dad stopped to pray with him, to show him love in the best way he knew how. Love shown, bit by bit, let's you know you are not alone.

[[callout: Love shown, bit by bit, let's you know you are not alone.]]

I don't think I would have made it without the love and the support of my family and friends. I was struggling, and I was terrified. I was nineteen years old, and the doctors were telling me that I had a diagnosis that meant I might have a few weeks to a few months to live. For the next few days, during my moments of coherence while I was undergoing every medical test known to man, all I could think of were the things I was never going to be able to do or experience. I'd never be an uncle and see my nieces and nephews. I'd never be able to get married and have children of my own. I thought about the son I'd never have and never get to play ball with, and I laid in my hospital bed and cried.

I don't have a lot of words to describe what that was like. As I said, my family is full of fighters and believers. We hadn't given up all hope, but it was a scary time. After I made it through my list of all the things I'd never get to do, I began to reflect on my life. I began to think about the people I'd wronged over the years. The ones I'd hurt and perhaps never given an adequate apology. I started a new list, and I began to do something about it.

I sent a message to every person I could think of. I asked forgiveness where it was needed, and I poured my heart out to my friends and family. Over the next several days after the diagnosis, as my numbers go worse and worse, I reached out to everyone I could to make amends. While I was reaching out to friends and family, they were reaching back to us in so many ways.

On Wednesday evening, our pastor called to say that after he started teaching during the evening service, he felt compelled to stop and have everyone pray for me. We found out there were several corporate prayers for me that night too. Entire congregations were praying, I was getting prayer texts and messages every single day. I knew people were praying for me, but on day twelve, things started to really blow up:

"Praying for you, Sam."
"You've got this, Sam."
"Nothing's impossible, Sam. We're praying."

I needed it. My mom compared us to a plane circling the airport during a storm—we needed the storm to cease because we were quickly running out of fuel. At that moment, my lymph node biopsies were being examined in labs at St. Louis and all over the country—MD Anderson, the Mayo Clinic, the Center for Disease Control. I kept getting sicker and we kept waiting.

Thursday dawned, and I was at my absolute worst. The whites of my eyes turned as yellow as my skin, and my numbers had their greatest downturn yet.

That day, my college coach and teammates came to see me. They learned more about the illness and realized just how dire my situation was. A couple of weeks before, I was a healthy, strong college baseball pitcher. And now I was wasting away, barely able to get out of my hospital bed. To this day, I don't know whose idea it was, but students at my college held a prayer vigil for me. During the Thursday evening, student-led worship service on campus, hundreds of college kids went that night and prayed for me. It was amazing. What was even more amazing was that it brought some people to the Lord. People who had been walking their own way rededicated their lives to Christ, and some were even saved for the first time. I started getting messages like, "Because of you, I came back to God." We were blown away. It was another amazing reminder that maybe this was not about us.

I was humbled and honored. But I have to admit; I was still so scared. One of our preachers came to pray for me; he was praying for my soul, almost like he was praying my last rites. I began to cry out to God with everything within me.

"God," I prayed, "I know you're there. And I know you've forgiven me of my sins and my selfishness. Please forgive me. Please forgive me for living for myself and not for You. If you want to take me home now, I understand. I do. But please, if you'll give me a second chance, I promise I'll live for you. I'll do better. I'll serve you and others and not let my life be all about me."

In two weeks I had lost 40 pounds, I was weak, and my jaundiced skin had gone from Dijon mustard yellow to nacho cheese yellow. It was bad. I prayed my heart out that night, and then I left it with Jesus and went to sleep.

The next morning, I woke feeling better. Quite a lot better. My dad had stayed with me that night so my mom could go back to the hotel and take a shower and try to get a little bit of sleep. When she walked in the next day, she first saw my dad's eyes—they were shining bright with hope.

"Mama, we had a good night!" he said. "A very good night!"

"Sam!" She said with glee. "You're pink! You're not the color of Gray Poupon!" She came over to my bed and burst into tears. She was thanking God and telling me how much she loved me and that my skinny self looked like a giraffe in a baby bed. We still had no updated results, but we had hope and laughter was bursting out of my hospital room.

Doctors and nurses kept showing up again and more tests started coming, only this time, I was feeling better, not worse.

My family and I will never, ever forget the moment the doctors came to tell us I did not have Castleman's disease. My mom was in the checkout line at the hospital cafeteria when my dad called to tell her to get back to the room—they had the results. She put down her breakfast and ran back to my room. That young resident was waiting and beaming ear to ear. This time, he got to deliver the good news.

My numbers had turned on a dime. They didn't have an explanation for the turn around. But we did. My numbers had turned on a prayer, or really the prayers of hundreds of friends, family members, church members, and fellow students. Pure, unadulterated relief and joy washed over each one of us. Praise God.

Days before, I was lying in a hospital bed physically weak and wasting away, fearing my death. And suddenly, my skinny self was dancing in my hospital room. The next day, I went home.

I don't know exactly why all of that happened to me, but I know God used it for good. I woke up and saw myself, really saw myself for the first time in well over a year.

During those two weeks of my illness, I was reminded that God had a plan for me and a purpose for my life. And that plan would be for His glory, not mine. Suddenly, I could see clearly again. I remembered a very important moment in my life, and I knew what I was supposed to be doing and who I was supposed to be helping.

I had lost my focus. I had taken my eye off the ball. But those weeks in the hospital took me back to that camp and those limb-different kids I was able to help. I remembered how the experience changed me. I remembered how much I enjoyed seeing those kids come alive when they let go of their fear and realized what they were capable of. And I remembered the vision I had about what I was supposed to do with my life—about how God wanted to use me and about who exactly I was supposed to be helping. The worst thing that ever happened to me took me back to the best thing that ever happened to me—realizing my purpose to help kids who struggle like I used to struggle, kids who might have a physical difference to deal with, but who are so capable of so much.

I had to lay down my pride and exchange it for God's plan and His redemption. It was the best trade I ever made. Letting go of pride and selfishness are life-long, daily acts of surrender. It's hard, but it's worth it. We have to get up every day and say, "Okay, Lord. Help me to see myself clearly and live for You instead of me; help me to have hands that offer grace to everyone I meet."

I promise, if you're willing to do that too, there's an adventure on the other side that's far better than living for yourself.

I left that hospital more determined than ever. Six months later, NubAbility held its very first camp.

Chapter 8

Live in Community and Be a Team Player

Life Is Best Lived With Loving, Supportive People By Our Sides

---

"For the strength of the pack is the wolf, and the strength of the wolf is the pack."

Rudyard Kipling

On July 22, 2012, I found myself on the softball field at Greenville College surrounded by my family and friends, seven limb-different coaches, and 19 campers and their families. It was the end of our very first NubAbility camp, and it was everything I had hoped it would be. We were learning and growing and figuring a few things out as we went along, but we were setting the foundation for something that was about to change our lives forever.

It was almost the end of camp, and we were taking the field for our all-player wiffle-ball game to close out the weekend. The kids were having so much fun, and they were all so excited to play. One of my first goals as a coach was to make sure I never, ever told any of the children that they couldn't do something. No matter what. I had my first test during this game when the cutest four-year-old you can imagine came up to me and said, "I want to bat!"

Sweet Zoe was born with no arms. Her family adopted her from China, and what she was lacking in the presence of her limbs, she was more than making up for in spunk and personality. I looked down at her and smiled, but I wasn't quite sure how to respond.

"I want to bat!" she said again, this time with more persistence. "Here," she said, motioning with her head and chin. I didn't know how this would work, but she was going to show me.

I reached over with the wiffle bat, and she tucked it between her chin and shoulder. "Okay, pitch to me!" she hollered, and the pitcher tossed the ball in her direction.

Whack! You should have seen her smack that ball with a bat that was tucked under her chin. It was remarkable! She took off running as someone started to field the ball. Without thinking, I scooped her up high on my shoulders and took off so she was out of reach of the tag. Zoe's belly laugh filled the air, and everyone began to cheer as we were chased around the bases. I plopped her down on home plate for her first homerun, and the 19 kids and their families, the coaches, and my family and friends cheered our heads off for her.

I think of all those faces and all the support wrapped up in that moment. All of those people who came together to learn, grow their skills, and help each other. We became a team that day. A strong community—a family.

In my experience, engaging ourselves with a supportive community is one of the best ways to live our lives and an essential practice of people who become game changers. It's a humbling reality to face, but we're just not that great on our own. We can only do so much, but when we're surrounded by a supportive community it's like being part of an incredible team. And when you're on a great team, you learn how to both give and receive so the team can be its absolute best.

Our first camp happened about eight months after my illness and hospitalization. In those months, I was learning the hard way all the things that can go wrong when we're too stubborn to ask for help and we don't embrace a supportive community. I thought I had released my pride in that hospital bed, but in some ways it was like it morphed into something that looked a little different but was still the same stinking issue of pride. I was no longer living entirely for myself or thinking I was entirely responsible for my successes. I was very aware of all that God had done for me. And grateful—I was so grateful for all of it. Yet, this new version of pride slipped into my life after I had laid down the old one, and I was convinced that I could a.) do it all, and b.) I could do it all by myself. I did not need to ask for help from anyone other than God.

Except that I really did need to ask for help. I really needed to engage with the loving, supportive team that surrounded me.

From my vantage point, it seems like our world is largely broken down into three types of people. The first type has it under control. They don't need help with anything. Ever. They are ultra-capable (a little proud), responsible (a little stressed), and they can always get the job done (okay, they're a lot stressed). They are superstars, but unfortunately, they're not always the best team players. The second type of people wants help with everything, even when they don't actually need it. They don't want to brush their teeth without assistance.

The world really needs more people in the third category. These few and remarkable souls are hard workers. They are exceptionally capable too. They can totally get the job done. But when life gets really hard, they are not so proud that they can't go to their close friends and family and say things like:

I'm really struggling. Would you pray for me?

I could really use help with _____.

I'm having a hard time, and I could use some advice and guidance.

I have this problem, and I was thinking through a few solutions. Could I discuss them with you?

These are the people who have figured out the secret of living in community, and they make the best teammates. What if we were the kind of people who both worked hard and knew how to get things done, but we also didn't have so much pride that we couldn't ask for help? Our lives and communities might just be transformed.

A lot of game changers fall into that third category. They work hard, but they don't work in silos. And they know how to identify when things will go a lot better if they ask for assistance, and then they do just that. Unfortunately, I had to learn this lesson the hard way after I got out of the hospital. I missed so much school with my illness. I was out for nearly a month. Some students might be able to handle that (or at least ask for help soon enough to keep them afloat), but with it being my first year of college and being an athlete on the baseball team, I spent the rest of the school year drowning in silence.

The crazy thing was, I was surrounded by people who would have been more than happy to help me. Thrilled even. They would have never wanted me to struggle the way that I was struggling. I knew for a fact my parents would be understanding about the situation and do anything to help me get this figured out. My roommate was a great guy, and he was super disciplined and responsible with his studies. He would have helped me in an instant if I'd asked. And my coaches, well they were awesome. I remember conversations at practices and early morning workouts:

"Hey, Sam, come over here," a coach would say. "How are you feeling? Looks like you're getting some strength back."

"Yep, thanks, Coach. Feeling good."

"Good, good. And how are your classes? That had to be hard being out sick for so long."

"Fine. Thanks. Everything's fine." And then I would slip away before my face gave away that things were not fine.

❖

I'll be the first one to tell you that I've never had a reputation as a studious, straight-A student. My academic goals boiled down to getting good enough grades to spend my life on the ball diamond. And when I accomplished that, I'd go spend most of my time playing ball or having a good time with my buddies.

But not that year. I was studying like crazy. I was convinced I could make up my time in the fall. I had withdrawn from school for the rest of the semester after my illness and had taken incompletes. Right before my spring semester, my parents had talked to my coaches and professors about how to best set up my schedule for success. We requested that my hardest classes be early in the morning, so I would miss them the least when I had baseball games. But when I got there and picked up my schedule, the opposite had happened.

"You know, I'll bet there's still time to fix this," my mom had said. "Let's just run down to the registrar's office and see if they have some other options."

"No, no. That's okay," I told her. "I can do it, Mom."

But then my professors from the fall reached out to me about completing my work from the first semester. I thought I could do both. Unfortunately, I was wrong, and by the time I finally asked for help, it was too late.

I'd played an amazing first season of college ball. It was awesome. And then I found out I was on academic probation, and my second season would be on hold.

Here are a few questions I wish I would have asked myself:

Why is it that I am refusing to ask for help?
What's the worst that could happen if I did?
Would I want someone I love to go through this experience and feel like they couldn't ask me for help?

When you find yourself buried in life, whether you dug the hole yourself or you ended up there by circumstances out of your control, these are great questions to think through. The last one in particular really gets me these days.

It gets me now because of kids like Zoe and all my other campers at NubAbility. These kids, in my opinion, are some of the most amazing children in the world. They've overcome incredible odds. I've seen children with no arms, children with no legs, children missing one of each, and children with so many other challenges—and these kids absolutely shine. They are so full of life it would blow your mind.

If I knew that one of them was afraid to ask for help or come and talk to someone about hard things they were facing, it would break my heart. I would never want that for them. If we wouldn't want those things for others, then we shouldn't put them on ourselves. If there's anything I've learned from life and baseball, it's that game changers can't be game changers by themselves. They have to be willing to ask for help, and they have to live in healthy community with others. Metaphorically, they have to be on a great team. Whether you're an athlete, artist, genius, missionary, entrepreneur, or something else, you need a community of people in your life. An active, caring community. If you're surrounded with that, it's possible that you really can do anything.

I missed out on some things, and I put way more pressure on myself than I ever needed to, but I learned some important lessons during that difficult season of life.

Top Five Ways Community Can Change Your Life

In my opinion, here are the top five ways living in community can change your life and help you be a game changer:

You need to be able to share your burdens. In the Bible, Jesus tells us that His yoke is easy, and His burden is light. Yokes don't mean a whole lot to people these days because most of us don't see them too often. A yoke is the heavy wooden beam or crosspiece that farmers lay on top of their cattle or oxen to pull plows, carts, or machinery.

For weights that are too heavy for one animal to bear, yokes were attached to two, and together they would carry the burden. When we're yoked with Jesus, He's carrying the majority of the load; our burden is light. In the same way, God gives us friends and family to come alongside us, yoke themselves next to us, and help us lift our burdens. Galatians 6:2 tells us, "Bear one another's burdens, and thereby fulfill the law of Christ" (nasb). I have to tell you, even when people can't fix everything for you, just knowing they are walking beside you makes a tremendous difference. This segues to the next point, because even when the people beside you can't fix the problem, it still matters that they are there.

You must know that you're not alone. Loneliness is one of the worst feelings in the world. Loneliness is sad and awful, and it can also be incredibly dangerous. If we aren't careful, loneliness can morph into hopelessness, and hopelessness can cause us to spiral to very dark places. In chapter four, we talked about how important it is to find someone safe to talk to, and I cannot stress this enough. We must find safe people to talk to. Absolutely. I'm going to say this again so I'm sure you heard me: We must find safe people to talk to about our both our joys and our sorrows.

[[callout: We must find safe people to talk to about our both our joys and our sorrows.]] I'm so saddened every time I hear about another person who has committed suicide. And it feels like we hear it all the time. Teenagers, celebrities, pastors. It's affecting people of all ages from all walks of life. I'm by no means a professional when it comes to mental or physical health, and I know some are dealing with biological health issues in their bodies that are incredibly hard to get under control. I'm not going to address any of that. What I am going to address, what I'm going to plead with you about, is to please go talk to someone safe and healthy when you find yourself struggling and especially when you start to feel alone. And when it feels too hard, I want you to think about this: who do you love most in this world? Your child, niece or nephew, sibling, spouse, or best friend? Would you want them to feel like you feel now? Would you want them to remain silent? Remember, if you don't want it for the people you love the most, don't subject yourself to it. When we speak about our struggles out loud with safe, trusted people, it can take some of the struggle's power away. And not only for us, for other people who are struggling.

I can tell you from experience that when someone comes alongside you and puts an arm around you and says, "I'm here. I'll be with you," it can change your life. Even when people can't fix it for you, it's life-changing to have people come sit in the pit with you. It's life-changing to know that you are not alone.

You can get so much more done than you ever could alone. Ever heard the saying, "Many hands make light work?" Well, that's true in just about every area of your life, whether you're doing the dishes, playing a sport, or building an orphanage. We need each other. In 1 Corinthians 12:12, Paul describes people in the church as different parts of the body: "For just as the body is one and has many members, all the members of the body, though many, are one body, so it is with Christ" (esv). We're all different and unique, and we work best together, not alone. No matter how awesome we think we are, we'll never go very far by ourselves. And because we're different, we're so much better. Let's think about these things for a minute. What if I were the greatest pitcher in the world? Or even the greatest pitcher who ever lived? A multiple time Cy Young winner. Well, if I didn't have eight other solid men standing with me, it doesn't matter how fast my fastball is, I'd still make up the world's crappiest baseball team. Eventually, someone's going to hit the ball, and I've got no one behind me to field it.

I think about NubAbility and how it's the thing I'm the proudest of—the thing I love the most. It would have never happened if it weren't for my mom who has taken it on like it's a full-time job and all of the other amazing people who give their time, talent, and energy to make it possible. Because a group of people chose to work together, limb-different children from all over the world get to grow their confidence, learn how to play sports, and open up amazing doors for their future. Amazing things we could never do all by ourselves are possible when we open ourselves to being a part of wonderful communities and teams.

You get to be a part of something bigger than yourself. We're all only going to get so many trips around the sun. The Bible tells us that from dust we came, and to dust we shall return. That's not fun to think about, but it should be something we spend some time thinking on because it reminds us how we should be living our lives. It makes us think more about God's plans, not our plans. It reminds us that it's not about us—it's about Him. And when we live and lead with that in mind, we can be a part of communities, organizations, and ministries that can long outlive us and continue to help people after we're gone.

You get to experience the joy of helping others. I'm going to let you in on a little secret. The whole point of being a game changer is not so you can change your own life—it's so you can change the lives of others. If we're only in this to make our lives better, to build our own accomplishments, and to achieve our own accolades—that kind of makes us jerks, not game changers. I know when we have a dream or a passion, or even if we're in a hard place, and we're trying to make our dreams come true to make life a little easier and give ourselves some space to breathe, it's easy to only think about ourselves. Especially when we're struggling. When we fall into survival mode, sometimes it's all we can do to get through the day. But our goal should always be to look forward, to look ahead. Keep moving and setting goals that will make a difference not only in your life, but also in the lives of others.

Does your dream somehow help others? Your job, your gift, your work? No matter what we do for a career, we can live lives of service to others. We can do it by supporting our churches and ministries and organizations throughout the world, and we can do it by waking up every day as game changers committed to living in community. When we live with this mindset, then we get to take part in everyday miracles:

We get to be the friend who puts our arms around another friend who is struggling. We take our turn shouldering the burden of the yoke and being with them in the pit.

We can show up and be someone's light in the darkness. We can make sure no matter what that person might be going through, he knows he is not alone. We can be the safe place for someone to share his problems.

We can make someone's work lighter. Whether we show up alone or with an army, we can help make the work lighter, faster, and more fun.

We can give our time, talent, and money and know that even if it was a small part we played, we had a role in things that matter, that were bigger than us, and might even outlive us. We can know the joy of living for something more than ourselves, for more than the moment.

We get to experience the indescribable joy of helping someone. God meant for us to take care of one another. And in His infinite wisdom, He must have known that not only would that help others and propel His purposes forward, it would fill our hearts with joy.

[[callout: The whole point of being a game changer is not so you can change your own life—it's so you can change the lives of others.]]

While I was struggling in silence, my mom was working like crazy to get our very first NubAbility camp off the ground. She was working tirelessly to get through all of the paperwork that's involved in setting up a non-profit organization. She was researching, networking, and reaching out to all kinds of people to help us. She knew it was something we could never accomplish entirely on our own, and she was willing to step out and ask for help, even when it was uncomfortable.

My mom was a high school teacher. She didn't have a marketing or business degree, and she'd never been the president of a non-profit organization. She'd never had to navigate the IRS, the Illinois Secretary of State, the Department of Revenue, or the Attorney General's office. But she was willing to step out into unfamiliar territory, ask questions, and get help when she needed it so that the dream of NubAbility could become a reality.

Because of the amazing people who came together with my mom and I, all was not lost at the end of that semester when I found out I would have to be on academic probation. Because on a beautiful weekend in June, NubAbility held its first camp. Note the capital A to emphasize the incredible Ability of each child who comes through our camp. The first 19 kids got to experience three days of camp and have their eyes opened to all that they were capable of. Zoe got to hit her first homerun.

It was all because a community of people came together.

Friends, we were never meant to live in silos, and we can't be silent in our struggles. We were meant to live in community, so that we can both help and be helped. So that we can comfort and be comforted.

May you be on the giving and receiving ends of a safe and loving community of people. May you be an incredible team player and live a life surrounded by amazing teammates. When we live lives like this, we get to fulfill this wonderful verse:

Praise be to the God and Father of our Lord Jesus Christ, the Father of compassion and the God of all comfort, who comforts us in all our troubles, so that we can comfort those in any trouble with the comfort we ourselves receive from God.

2 Corinthians 1:3–4 NIV.

Chapter 9

Be Willing to Show up and Let God Use You

When We Make Ourselves Available, We Open Up The Door Of Opportunity To Be Part Of God's Divine Purposes

---

"Let God have your life; He can do more with it than you can."

D.L. Moody

As our camp continued each year, I did everything I could do to make sure each child had a coach with the same or similar difference as well as a shared sport. I have to tell you, this wasn't always easy.

One year, we had a new girl coming to camp. She was six years old, and she had only one arm and one leg. Her name was Brooklyn, and she wanted to be a basketball player. I searched high and low for someone in a similar situation to coach her, and I couldn't find anyone. Finally, my mom told me, "It's okay, Sam. It will be alright. The coaches we have will still be a huge help to her." I knew that was true, but I had really wanted to find the right person. To me, the right person was a basketball player with one arm and one leg.

Camp day rolled around, and we were all so excited to get started. So many people show up every year to help us get these camps off the ground, and it's always amazing to me to see what happens when people make themselves available and let God use them. Dion, a guy from my hometown, is one of our camp heroes. Every year, he drives a limo back and forth to the St. Louis airport to pick everyone up. It's an hour and a half one way, and he makes multiple trips a day carrying people back and forth. In a limo, no less! And he does this for us completely as a gift to NubAbility. He's amazing.

On this particular year, our hero Dion went to pick up a motivational speaker who was coming to share her story with the kids and inspire them. Ashley was not only an amputee, but she also had a health condition that caused calcification of certain parts of her body. We didn't know it at the time, but she needed her assistant to travel with her. When she arrived, she started a conversation with my mom about how a young woman had traveled with her and that she would need her help while she was at the hotel, but we were welcome to have her assist with the kids at camp the rest of the time.

"I'd like you to meet Whitney," Ashley said, as Dion opened the limo door. And then out climbed a fit and athletic woman with one arm and one leg. "You know, she was a basketball player in college," Ashley continued to my mom. When I approached the scene and saw Whitney, my jaw hit the pavement.

"What's going on?" I stammered. "How? Who is that?" I couldn't believe it. It's like sometimes God answers prayers we have in our hearts but forget to say out loud. But there was Whitney.

Exactly who we needed, right when we needed her. I asked for her help with Brooklyn and she didn't even hesitate to step up. She said yes. She made herself available. She showed up and let God use her.

We raced to find Brooklyn. We could not wait to introduce her to her new coach. Later that day during our opening ceremonies, Brooklyn's mom stood in the bleachers with tears streaming down her face. Her daughter now had an incredible opportunity to be taught and coached by someone who knew exactly what her struggles were and who was able to help her find ways to overcome them.

Have you ever had something like that happen? You don't have to be a limb-different person to have had an experience where you felt like God sent someone to you right in the moment when you needed that person in your life. You might have had a shared experience that helped you overcome your past, or it might be a mentor that's going to help you as you move forward to your future. It might be both. When those amazing moments happen to us, it's important for us to remember it was because someone was willing to be available. Someone was willing to show up.

I don't think these experiences are chance encounters or coincidences. I think when we make ourselves available, we open up the door of opportunity to be part of God's divine purposes. We might not ever know the full impact of our presence, but every now and then, we get a glimpse.

Mason was a great friend of mine and an all-around great guy. I met him my first year at Greenville college, and from the second he heard about my vision for NubAbility, he bought into it immediately. He was sold on it before anything had ever happened with an actual camp.

"I'm there, man," I remember him saying. And he wasn't lying. He showed up for me again and again.

Mason was the quarterback on the football team and a very popular guy on campus. He had plenty to keep him busy during our college years, but he made our NubAbility camp a priority and showed up to help me for years.

His first camp also happened to be Zoe's first camp. Remember Zoe? My homerun slugger who was born without arms?

Zoe's family drove her more than seven hours to get her to NubAbility camp. She was a four-year-old little girl the first time we met her. When she laid eyes on Mason, she found a friend for life.

Zoe had come to learn gymnastics, but just like she'd been so intent to bat, she had also been completely determined to learn how to play football. She latched on to both Mason and his sport; it didn't seem to bother her at all that she didn't have arms. She was going to find a way to play football. And find a way she did.

Mason and Zoe became a dynamic duo. Mason figured out how he could hike the ball to Zoe such that she could catch it with her feet. She would then tee up the ball with her toe so a kicker could launch it. She was in her element. She loved it so much; our faces were splitting with smiles as we watched her light up over her newfound skill.

Over and over and over again. Mason would hike the ball; Zoe would catch it and tee it up; and then a kicker would send it sailing. And then to everyone's delight she'd holler, "Do it again, white boy! Do it again!"

For three days, Mason was Zoe's personal coach, trainer, and jungle gym. She was constantly riding on his back, and if ever he got out of her sight, she was asking for him. It was such a cool thing to watch. Later, after camp ended, we all got together to recap and talk about what went right. We were all feeling great and overwhelmed with how amazing it was to help these kids. Everyone was smiling and having a great time when we looked over and saw that Mason was crying.

Quarterbacks don't cry that often, so when he started to speak, we were listening.

"I just have to thank you all so much for letting me be here. You will never know how much it meant to me to help that little girl and see how much joy she got from playing ball." He went on, "And I have to tell you something. I have had an aversion to feet my entire life. Seriously, I've always hated them. I've never really talked about this to anyone, but feet have always bothered me. I don't like them at all; I don't like to see them or touch them, and I've always cleaned my toenails like crazy. It was like God healed me of that these last few days. My foot issue didn't matter at all in light of helping Zoe. She's such an amazing kid, and I can't believe how fun this was."

One of my favorite things about camp is having a front-row seat to see so many of these coaches and kids have such amazing impacts on each other. I'm so glad Mason showed up for that camp and for the many camps after. I learned from him how a willingness to be available for God can change others in incredible ways. And it can change us and help us in ways we would have never imagined.

My experiences with NubAbility and seeing how others have been so willing to show up and let God use them have taught me a few things I need to continually work on in my own life:

I need to pray more. It always amazes me how often I forget to pray. When I need a coach like Whitney. When I need help. When I should be asking for opportunities to serve Him. If you want to be used by God, just ask. John 15:7 says, "If you abide in me, and my words abide in you, ask whatever you wish, and it will be done for you" (esv). A few definitions of abide can be defined as "to observe, to follow, to keep, to hold to, or to stand by." When we're focused on abiding with God, I think our prayers are more likely to be prayers that honor him. I'm so confident that when I ask with a pure heart and sincere intention, "God, please use me. Show me how I can serve you and who you want me to help," I know without a doubt He's listening. And I can't wait to see how He's going to answer.

I need to be still more. I need to be still both in the holy sense of spending quiet time devoted to God, and I also need to be still in the sense that I simply need to pay more attention to what's happening around me. We are surrounded by hurting people, and we have to stop and see them. Unfortunately, sometimes we're so busy, we let them go right on by without even noticing. We are too busy to hear God's voice and too busy to see the pain in the eyes of the people around us. We have to keep our eyes open so we can see what's really going on. When you ask people how they are doing, stop, look into their faces, and listen to their answers.

A friend of mine once told me a story about a dark time in her life when her family was facing a serious illness. For months, when people asked how she was, she'd say, "I'm okay," because it seemed the best thing she could say without lying. She was still breathing, so she reasoned that she was okay. One day, on her way to the hospital, she stopped at the Starbucks drive-thru. When the man on the other end of the speaker asked how she was, she answered her customary, "I'm okay."

And then to her amazement, he answered her, full of compassion with, "Why are you just okay?"

She'd been feeling so overlooked for so long, it caught her off guard; she immediately got choked up and stammered, "Well, I'm on my way to the hospital today."

"Oh, I'm sorry to hear that. Your coffee is on me then."

She still can't tell this story without crying. Because someone took two minutes out of his day to really see her and buy her a cup of coffee.

How many times a day are we missing those moments when God could use us? It might only cost us two minutes and a cup of coffee. When we slow down and let ourselves be still, we can hear God and see others more clearly.

I need to be willing to try new things and sometimes be uncomfortable. One year, the girls in our tumbling group who were practicing their cartwheels requested that I join them and try too. I mean, a cartwheel, right? I can do that. I was convinced that wouldn't be a problem, and that as their fearless leader, I should encourage them to keep trying and keep honing their skills. Unfortunately, I only provided entertainment. My first cartwheel became my last cartwheel when I landed on my face.

And then last year, the girls who came to camp to practice dance wanted to teach me their routine. They thought I should also join the dance group. (They were wrong.)

You guys. It's for the children. Be willing to try new things and be uncomfortable. That's all I'm saying. That and I'm sticking with baseball.

I need to be open. My mother wakes up every single day and says, "Okay, Lord. How can I serve you today?" And she stays quite busy serving him in amazing ways. I've learned in my own life, when I'm open to God and open with others, awesome things can happen. A few years ago, I met a guy at Pirate Camp, and we sat down around another bonfire to talk. (In case you're wondering, Pirate Camp is a water sports camp for limb-different kids. No peg-legs required. Clever, right? The kids love it, and who doesn't want to be a pirate?) He looked over and said, "So what's giving you that glow?" He wasn't talking about flames and the glowing firelight. I decided to be open and take a chance. I started sharing my faith, and as it happened, he was a believer, too, and we spent the next four hours talking about Jesus. Today, this man who experienced a traumatic amputation is one of our amazing camp partners. We work with him all the time at our Florida camps as he helps limb-different children with water sports. You just never know what kind of doors God's going to open when you live your life being willing and open. And when we feel like we might be opening up ourselves to help others, a lot of times God is using those moments to help us.

I need to show up more. We don't always need to overthink things. Sometimes we just need to show up. Whitney showed up. Mason showed up. One time, I was visiting a camp in Florida as their motivational speaker. The day after I had given my talk to the campers and their families, I found myself in the lunchroom getting ready to eat. I had my lunch in hand and my sights set on a lone rocking chair, but as I headed that direction, I felt like God was saying, "I didn't bring you here to seclude yourself." So, I did an about-face and headed to the crowded picnic tables. Before I could sit and take a bite, one of the mamas came right at me. "I've been looking for you everywhere! I run orphanages in Haiti for limb-different children." Not only did this woman found and run several orphanages in Haiti, but she also had adopted her son from there. Gesnel was a young teen who was so full of life. He had a condition that caused an enormous tumor on his arm, and he had only nubs for fingers on that hand. We had been looking for a child to send to one of our NubAbility camps on full scholarship, and after talking with her, I knew Gesnel was the one.

Getting there was no easy feat for Gesnel and his mom. They had every flight delay and cancelation you could imagine. And when they finally arrived in St. Louis, a wrong turn had them heading down the highway in the wrong direction. Everything was working against this kid, but finally, he made it to our camp.

Today, Ges is excelling in so many areas. At our camp he learned that his skill in soccer was good enough for school and elite league play. His confidence in his talents and gifts soared. He also learned from his limb-different coaches and mentors that he also could be just that for younger children in his mother's orphanages in Haiti. Ges is a senior in H.S. and has chosen to be homeschooled so he can travel back to Haiti often with his mom to help her in the orphanages. He is a very talented artist and now a junior coach in Soccer for NubAbility. It's amazing how God makes our paths cross with people at just the right time.

About the second year of our camp, a local youth pastor named Greg reached out to us about helping. This pastor was passionate about Jesus and passionate about sports. As a teenager, he started buying and selling sports memorabilia to raise money for mission trips. He wanted to help us, and the first year he was there, not only did he offer his time and energy, but he made sure each child left with a Jim Abbott baseball card.

What I didn't know back then was that his wife had just miscarried a baby. As he continued to come year after year, his wife Courtney began to join him. Over the years, they kept showing up at our camp and letting God use them. They also kept miscarrying babies.

One of the coolest things about our camp is that we are incredibly diverse. Kids from all over the world show up, and we always have a great group of kids—children who were biologically born to their parents with a limb difference, children who had a traumatic accident, and children who were born with a limb difference and then adopted. We happen to have a huge China adoption community.

One year at camp, Courtney and Greg looked at each other and said, "Hey. Why don't we go to China and adopt a limb-different child?"

Their daughter Emmie is so unbelievably cute, hilarious, and wise beyond her years. She is the biggest bundle of joy you can imagine. Courtney and Greg thought they were showing up to let God use them, and He absolutely did, but in the process, he opened doors and answered prayers that ended up being some of their greatest, most extravagant blessings they could have ever imagined. Before long, they'll be home with their second baby from China.

Here's the thing. I'm a different person because the game changers in my life have shown up. Even if you are the person who's been cut from every team you've tried out for or you missed the game-winning goal or you didn't get that amazing job or you feel like you don't have anything to offer, God wants to work through you. Someone needs you to show up. Someone's waiting for his or her life to be changed because of your willingness.

And because our God is so big and his grace and love are so unimaginably extravagant, just watch and see how He blesses you. Even the smallest, most insignificant situations can be used to glorify God if we make our lives about the real MVP.

Let's keep showing up.

Chapter 10
Trust God
And Let Him Take Care Of The Details

Trust in the Lord, and do good;
   dwell in the land and befriend faithfulness.
Delight yourself in the Lord,
   and he will give you the desires of your heart.
Commit your way to the Lord;
   trust in him, and he will act.
He will bring forth your righteousness as the light,
   and your justice as the noonday.
Be still before the Lord and wait patiently for him.

Psalm 37:3–7 esv

I've learned over the years that I need to trust God's plan, even when I have no idea what to do or what might happen in my future. This is pretty easy when things are moving right along and it seems like everything is going my way. It's less easy when things are tough. When clouds roll in and the sky gets dark, it's hard to see what's around the bend.

Life is like learning to pilot a plane. I'm sitting in the cockpit sweating the route and all the details and am all worried about the weather and visibility. But if I'm trusting God, I don't need to worry about any of that because He has the plane on autopilot. He knows exactly what's beyond the clouds and through the fog. He knows what's coming. He's got both the good and the bad times covered.

113

And He's guiding me through it. I think He also has a sense of humor and enjoys happy surprises; I think He likes to delight His children so there will be some amazing views, and so much of it will be an incredible ride.

I may not know the future, but I know the One who holds it. My job is to trust Him and to remain faithful. He's never let me down.

My all-time favorite Bible story is about Daniel and the lion's den from Daniel chapter six. The Bible describes Daniel as a person who lived his life being faithful to both God and man. I'm going to pair this with another favorite passage, the portion of Psalm 37 at the beginning of this chapter. I think there's so much we can learn from these scriptures.

While the Jews were living in exile, Daniel rose to power in spite of the fact that they were living in a foreign kingdom. King Darius the Mede became the ruler and decided to divide the kingdom into 120 provinces. He appointed an officer to rule over each, and then he chose Daniel and two others to rule over the officers and protect the King's interests. Because Daniel was so capable—and proved himself more capable than all of the officers—the King began to make plans to put him over the entire empire. Daniel was living a life that really epitomizes verse three: "Trust in the Lord, and do good; dwell in the land and befriend faithfulness."

Unfortunately, Daniel's good behavior and success didn't exactly win him a lot of friends among his fellow officers. Instead, the other officers were jealous, and they began to search for something that would take Daniel down. They found nothing. The New Living Translation says of Daniel in verse four: "He was faithful, always responsible, and completely trustworthy."

Now before we go any further in the story, let's pause here and think about that for a minute. Talk about something to aspire to! Is that how people would describe you and me? Faithful, always responsible, and completely trustworthy? It's worth noting that even his enemies could not find one negative fault to use against him. That right there is a testament of character. The people who were jealous of Daniel and couldn't stand him couldn't find a single thing wrong with him. He was living a game-changing life.

Back to the story. Once his fellow officers discovered there was not even a speck of dirt they could dig up on him, they knew they would have to concoct a plan. And because they knew Daniel was a man of character, they also knew it would have to be a trap. They concluded that the only way they could accuse him of something would be in regard to the rules of his religion.

Daniel prayed to God every single day, multiple times a day, and they all knew it. Verses six through nine share the brilliant idea they took to the king:

"Long live King Darius! We are all in agreement—we administrators, officials, high officers, advisers, and governors—that the king should make a law that will be strictly enforced. Give orders that for the next thirty days any person who prays to anyone, divine or human—except to you, Your Majesty—will be thrown into the den of lions. And now, Your Majesty, issue and sign this law so it cannot be changed, an official law of the Medes and Persians that cannot be revoked." So King Darius signed the law.

History is full of weird stuff. I read that and wonder, what in the world was he thinking? Based on other things the Bible says about him, he was seemingly not the most arrogant of rulers. He trusted Daniel, after all. Surely, he had something better to do than sign such ridiculous laws into place, right? Apparently not. Pride and power can be a terrible combination.

Here's another game-changing moment from Daniel: when he learned about the new law, he continued to remain faithful to

115

God. And did you see that the law was only for 30 days? Would we have rationalized, well, it's only 30 days . . . I'll pray again in 30 days . . . or I'll pray silently for the next 30 days and keep it a secret. Let's go back to the Psalm for a minute. Verse five says: "Commit your way to the Lord; trust in him, and he will act."

Daniel continued to commit his way to the Lord. He didn't let a change of his circumstances or a change of his culture alter him or his beliefs. Do we do that? Is our foundation on the Word of God or on the changing morality of our culture? God's Word stands forever, but culture, and it's ever-evolving standards, are shifting sands. Daniel stood firm, and he trusted God even when it was hard. Even when it was life or death.

Verses ten through fourteen of Daniel 6 tell us what happened next:

But when Daniel learned that the law had been signed, he went home and knelt down as usual in his upstairs room, with its windows open toward Jerusalem. He prayed three times a day, just as he had always done, giving thanks to his God. Then the officials went together to Daniel's house and found him praying and asking for God's help. So they went straight to the king and reminded him about his law. "Did you not sign a law that for the next thirty days any person who prays to anyone, divine or human—except to you, Your Majesty—will be thrown into the den of lions?"

"Yes," the king replied, "that decision stands; it is an official law of the Medes and Persians that cannot be revoked."

Then they told the king, "That man Daniel, one of the captives from Judah, is ignoring you and your law. He still prays to his God three times a day."

Hearing this, the king was deeply troubled, and he tried to think of a way to save Daniel. He spent the rest of the day looking for a way to get Daniel out of this predicament.

King Darius is an interesting person. I wish we were all a lot more like Daniel but so often, we're living more like Darius. Some days we're doing okay, making good choices. And then we do something epically stupid. Pride, arrogance, selfishness—something gets in the way that causes to make a really dumb decision. Before we know it, we're working like crazy to dig ourselves out of a disastrous hole of our own making.

No matter how hard he tried, Darius couldn't get himself out of this particular pit. He left no loophole for himself in the absurd law he signed into fruition. And Daniel was on his way to the lion's den. Verse fifteen begins:

In the evening the men went together to the king and said, "Your Majesty, you know that according to the law of the Medes and the Persians, no law that the king signs can be changed."

So at last the king gave orders for Daniel to be arrested and thrown into the den of lions. The king said to him, "May your God, whom you serve so faithfully, rescue you."

A stone was brought and placed over the mouth of the den. The king sealed the stone with his own royal seal and the seals of his nobles, so that no one could rescue Daniel. Then the king returned to his palace and spent the night fasting. He refused his usual entertainment and couldn't sleep at all that night.

Thankfully, the Lord forgives us for our offenses if and when we repent, but we often still have to pay the consequences for our actions. Interestingly enough, Daniel was the one in the pit, but it sounds like Darius was the one sweating it out over his choices.

Very early the next morning, the king got up and hurried out to the lions' den. When he got there, he called out in anguish, "Daniel, servant of the living God! Was your God, whom you serve so faithfully, able to rescue you from the lions?"

Daniel answered, "Long live the king! My God sent his angel to shut the lions' mouths so that they would not hurt me, for I have been found innocent in his sight. And I have not wronged you, Your Majesty."

The king was overjoyed and ordered that Daniel be lifted from the den. Not a scratch was found on him, for he had trusted in his God.

Did you catch that last line? For he had trusted in his God. Storms of life come to everyone. I think sometimes we might get scratches even when we are trusting God. But in this case, the sentence connects the fact that not a scratch was found on him to his trust in God. As again in verse five from Psalm 37, he trusted in God, and God acted on his behalf.

Remember what we said about consequences? The other officers are about to pay for their crimes. And not only them, but also their entire families:

Then the king gave orders to arrest the men who had maliciously accused Daniel. He had them thrown into the lions' den, along with their wives and children. The lions leaped on them and tore them apart before they even hit the floor of the den.

Then King Darius sent this message to the people of every race and nation and language throughout the world:

"Peace and prosperity to you!
I decree that everyone throughout my kingdom should tremble with fear before the God of Daniel.
For he is the living God,
    and he will endure forever.
His kingdom will never be destroyed,
    and his rule will never end.
He rescues and saves his people;
    he performs miraculous signs and wonders
    in the heavens and on earth.
He has rescued Daniel
    from the power of the lions."

So Daniel prospered during the reign of Darius and the reign of Cyrus the Persian.

The end of our passage from Psalm 37 tells us: He will bring forth your righteousness as the light, and your justice as the noonday. Both Daniel's righteousness and justice were brought before the light, and not only that, but His God was given glory and honor throughout the land. Because of how Daniel lived his life, Darius, a foreign king, sent a declaration about Daniel's God to every person and race and nation in the world.

And finally, let me go back a few verses in that Psalm. Verse four tells us: "Delight yourself in the Lord, and he will give you the desires of your heart." I'm saving that one for the end, because the end of Daniel 6 says, "So Daniel prospered during the reign of Darius and the reign of Cyrus the Persian." Now, do I think this means that if we delight ourselves in the Lord, we'll be rich, successful, and life will always be easy? No, I don't think that, and that's not what the Bible says. I do think that if we delight ourselves in the Lord, He'll be at work in our hearts and shape them to have desires that are good and that glorify Him. And if you look up the definition of prosper, some sources say that to prosper is to flourish, thrive, or do well. I think that's likely what Daniel did. And I think if we trust in the Lord and do good, if we delight ourselves in Him and live faithful lives of character—though hard times will come— we, too, will flourish, thrive, and do well.

I've endured several dark seasons in my life where I needed to trust God. Some of those seasons happened because I was like Darius, and I ended up in a pit of my own making. And for some, I was like Daniel. Trying to do the right thing when life happened and got hard. Sometimes I ended up in the middle of both at the same time. Trusting God and shifting my focus to Him has always been the thing that has gotten me through. He has acted on my behalf in ways that I wasn't expecting, and he's taken some challenging situations and worked them out for my good.

That first summer after my freshman year, when I ended up on academic, probation and off the team for a year, I was so disappointed. Disappointed in myself for not getting help and making the grades I needed and disappointed that I had to put my baseball dream on hold for an entire season.

And then, to top that off, I found out I needed foot surgery. My foot had really been bothering me for a while; I had done something to it during the season, and it was causing me a lot of pain. My season ended, I was handed academic probation, and I thought, what the heck, I might as well go get my foot fixed. Only, it wasn't an easy fix. Strangely enough, I was born with no left hand but an extra bone in my foot. The main tendon that runs down the front of the leg was attached to my extra bone instead of the bone it was supposed to be attached. As a bonus, I had broken my extra bone. One complicated surgery, three months on crutches and a scooter, and 90 days in a boot later . . . I was mostly better.

I couldn't play ball first because of my academic probation—and then come to find out—I wouldn't have been able to any way because of my foot. I decided to transfer to the junior college back home for a year and focus on my grades, my family, and NubAbility. This was no pit of lions by any stretch of the imagination; it was just not at all how I thought my freshman year of college would go. But it taught me that I had to trust God. When things go right, when things go wrong, when I have no idea how things are going to go next—I need to trust God.

The year I spent at my local community college was good in many ways; I worked hard at my studies, and I continued to practice so I could get back to baseball. As it turned out, I made it back to baseball, but not back to Greenville. Do you remember the coach I mentioned in the first chapter? Well, he showed up again. This time to ask if I wanted to be on the baseball team of a new college. He wanted me to be a leader to help pioneer the new team. I said yes. I would get one more season in the sun as a college baseball player.

Life can have a lot of surprises, and for better or worse, things don't always turn out how we expect. But Daniel's life shows us how game changers are steady and faithful. Here are a few of my favorite things to remember about his story:

Game changers are people of character. Daniel was such a man of character that even his enemies couldn't find fault in him. That's pretty amazing right there. Are our lives so faithfully consistent, that if people were watching us closely—looking for things we are doing wrong—they wouldn't be able to find anything? And instead, they would see people who are faithful and consistent in prayer and seeking God? People who are trustworthy and who have won the respect of their employers? Like they knew to find Daniel, facing Jerusalem, and bowed in prayer three times a day, do people know to find us in a posture of faithfulness and in worship to our God?

Game changers are steady and faithful to God's Word. This one is tough too. Are we faithful to God and His Word when culture changes? When following God and the tenets of the Bible are no longer popular or politically correct? Or legal? The new "law" of Daniel's land was in direct opposition to God. Our culture today is often in direct opposition to God's Word. How do we respond? Are we brave enough to stick to God's laws when it could get us in trouble? And as we process through this and think through why we do some of the things we do, it's important to ask ourselves hard questions. Are we trying to merely be good, or are we trying to be found faithful and trustworthy to the One who never changes?

Game changers trust. I think it's interesting that the Bible doesn't really say much from Daniel's point of view in this story until after he's rescued from the den of lions. It tells us that Darius is fretting all night, but it doesn't tell us what Daniel is doing. I'm an animal guy, personally, and I'd like to think he was snuggled up with the lions like my dogs snuggle up beside me. Assuming he wasn't allergic to cats, I'd like to think it was a warm, peaceful, and restful evening and that he and the giant kitties had a nice snooze. That's a great visual, but all joking aside, we know his peace wasn't found in a cuddly cat. It was found in the presence of God, in the presence of the angel sent by God to keep the lions' mouths closed and to keep God's servant Daniel safe.

I believe God's presence can be experienced at any time. But it seems to me He often shows up in the pits and in the storms. When, without Him, His children would be frantic with fear. But with His presence comes peace. And where there is trust and peace, there is security.

Game changers remain faithful. I both love and am in awe of Daniel's response to Darius when he came out of the lions' den. Darius asked "Daniel, servant of the living God! Was your God, whom you serve so faithfully, able to rescue you from the lions?" And Daniel replied: "Long live the king!" I would like to believe I would have emerged from that den with the same level of kindness and respect, but I'm sorely afraid my response would have been more like, "Yes, you idiot! What were you thinking?!" Not Daniel. He exited his trial with the same faithfulness and respect that he had entered it with.

Game changers think about whom they're listening to, and then game changers think it through. What if Darius had been paying attention? We have voices coming at us from everywhere—social media, advertisers, bullies, and a lot of people who likely don't have our best interest in mind. Frankly, we don't need to listen to a lot of them. Maybe most of them. We need to be discerning and focus on what God is saying and what the people who really care about our well-being are saying. If Darius had recognized that the voices coming at him were from petty men who were self-serving and jealous, the whole situation could have been avoided in the first place.

I know it feels like there's a whole lot to worry about, and I know there are a lot of voices coming at us. Sometimes we do stupid things like Darius. And sometimes it seems like life is hard for no reason at all. The best we can do is slide over and let God pilot our planes, trust him, and live faithful lives of character.

Chapter 11

Realize Your Weaknesses Can Be Your Biggest Strengths

Our Weaknesses Are Really Superpowers In The Hands Of God

Try to look at your weakness and convert it into your strength. That's success.

Zig Ziglar

Remember how I used to be the kid who walked around with his nub tucked into his pocket? I was afraid, ashamed, and so aware of the weakness that I carried around on the end of my left arm. I didn't realize that it was actually a strength. Probably one of my greatest.

I don't do that anymore. The Bible tells us to put away childish things as we grow. 1 Corinthians 13:11 says, "When I was a child, I talked like a child, I thought like a child, I reasoned like a child. When I became a man, I put the ways of childhood behind me" (niv).

People tend to have a variety of things they need to outgrow. We've talked about my long and winding road to get to a place where I was able to put my childhood ways of fear and shame

124

behind me. One of the ways I keep "the ways of childhood behind me" is that I actively do the opposite of some of my childhood struggles and habits. Remember how I always kept my nub hidden in my pocket? Now, when I'm out and about, particularly when I'm traveling, I make a point to wear my favorite shirt. It says: "I got 99 problems but the nub ain't one." I'm not ashamed now, so my nub isn't hidden away.

[[callout: Now, when I'm out and about, particularly when I'm traveling, I make a point to wear my favorite shirt. It says: "I got 99 problems but the nub ain't one."]]

Instead of being afraid of what people might be thinking of me, I'm excited about how I might have the opportunity to help and inspire people. I know from experience that there are people all over the world who could benefit from a conversation about being limb-different. Who knows when I'll meet the next game-changing coach, a kid who needs to be at our camp, or a donor who will support us in a way that allows us to change even more lives? If I'm not bold and open about who I am, how can these people find me?

Proudly displaying my nub also opens doors to help other people make better choices. It used to be that when I walked through airports, malls, or pretty much anywhere outside of my home, I was opening myself up to myriads of stares, whispers, and not-so-subtle finger pointing. If there's anything that feeds shame and fear, it's knowing that people are whispering and pointing.

Well, now my shirt says it loud and clear. No need to whisper. Let's have a conversation about it. Since I'm no longer afraid, and my nub is no longer my greatest weakness—it's my greatest strength to help others—let's talk about it. Out loud. Because maybe, just maybe, this will help others who are different in some way to endure fewer whispers, stares, and finger points.

Own Your Weakness . . . And Move On

A couple months after my illness I had the opportunity to travel with my college baseball team to the Dominican Republic. We were going for both missions and baseball, and I was so glad I was well enough to go. We got to go serve and help others and play baseball. I thought it might be the chance of a lifetime, and I was right. In addition to the opportunity to play ball with their incredibly talented teams, we were also able to bring much-needed supplies. When our cars would no longer make it down the muddy roads leading to the orphanages and sugar cane villages, we took turns carrying 50-pound bags of rice, bagged water, and beans for three miles. I thought I was going to go to play ball and help them, but they taught me so much.

Up until that point in my life, I was quite certain that people in the Midwest liked baseball. Compared to people in the Dominican? Not even close. The Dominican Republic was literally a whole different ball game. They love baseball. It is life. It is air. It is everything to them.

I remember walking down city streets that were basically in shambles. Old buildings, old cars, and dirty roads were everywhere. You know what else was everywhere? People crowded around storefronts anywhere there was an old color television. And when I say old, I mean like 1970s and 1980s dinosaur TV sets. These were sets we couldn't even find in thrift stores because they've all been trashed for a decade or two. But to these people, these televisions were gold, because baseball games were playing on them. And where there was baseball, the people of the Dominican were there watching.

Even though we were playing against their local teams, the crowds that came out to watch us were incredible, and they kept cheering for all of us. We got to play baseball for people who were overjoyed to be watching baseball. I think they were more excited about seeing us play ball than my Nana. It was one of the coolest sports experiences of my career, and it became one of my all-time favorite things that has ever happened to me on a ball field.

We were playing a game one afternoon on the trip; it was hot, and we were baking in the sun, but we could still feel and hear the ocean breezes blowing in from the sea. The small Caribbean nation is beautiful; it was like we were playing baseball in paradise.

My coach told me to go warm up, so I headed out to the bullpen, which was little more than a sandy patch of dirt past left field. The fields were old and run down; the outfield fence was a falling down concrete wall that looked like something out of a warzone. My catcher and I got set, and I start throwing. Suddenly, his eyes opened super wide. I stayed in position and started my motion to throw again when his hand came up to stop me. He motioned behind me. When I turned around, the entire crowd had gathered around us to watch. At first I got a little nervous, but then I noticed that their faces were in awe. These people were absolutely enamored with me. As proud as I was of my fastball, I knew that wasn't what stopped them in their tracks.

You see, in developing nations like the Dominican, limb-different children are often cast away, shunned, or given up for adoption. Some countries view such weaknesses and differences as plagues or curses, not gifts. It was probably the case that most of these people had never seen a limb-different person because they were not a part of regular society. And yet, in that moment they were definitely not shunning me.

My catcher and I eventually got back to our warm-up pitches, and then I made my way to the mound. Thankfully, I managed to step up to the rubber and throw a one-two-three inning. When strike three soared past the third batter, the crowd went nuts. They went so crazy they actually stormed the field, and I was suddenly surrounded by a mob of brand-new fans and friends who wanted my picture and my autograph and thought I was some type of miraculous hero. I was uneasy at first, but when they got to me, I felt like a celebrity. I suddenly found myself high-fiving and hugging strangers like they were friends I'd known for years.

It still makes me smile when I think of it. What makes me smile even more is the thought that maybe my presence changed the way someone thought about differences and so-called weaknesses. Maybe it caused someone else to get a second look or a second chance because these people had the opportunity to see what they might have once thought was a weakness could actually be a strength.

If I had never owned my weakness and moved past it as a child and teenager, I would have never had the opportunity to set foot on that mound. If I hadn't pushed beyond what most everyone ever thought I'd be able to do, I wouldn't have had the chance to show up at that moment in time.

Weaknesses come in all shapes and sizes. Sometimes we're born with them, sometimes we cause them, and sometimes we pick them up from others. It would be great if we only had one, but most of us have several. When it comes to using them as strengths, we'll never get anywhere if we don't own them first.

Have you ever known an alcoholic who was convinced he didn't have a drinking problem? For every second he stays in that place of denial, he's losing time toward changing his life and using his weakness as a strength to help others. Ever known a recovering alcoholic who has been to AA and through the twelve-step program and who helps others as a sponsor? Or who lives his or her life as an everyday miracle and testimony to show others what is possible?

This is a much smaller example, but for my entire school career, I got in trouble for talking. Pretty much every single day of my life a teacher had to tell Sam Kuhnert to be quiet. Now I'm a coach and motivational speaker—it's my job to talk. That's worked out pretty well for me so far. Sometimes our weaknesses are only weaknesses in our current context. They might be strengths in disguise.

This goes way beyond limb-differences, addictions, or my inability to be quiet. Your weaknesses might be any number of things, but whatever our weaknesses are, I've learned that we must own them. Otherwise, they will own us. And it doesn't matter how big or small they are. So many things in life can have a snowball effect. We want to do everything we possibly can to get the snowballs moving and growing in our favor. Name your weakness and own it. Then you can move on to find a solution.

Be a Problem Solver

I'm sure you've heard the saying, "Necessity is the mother of all invention." Sometimes amazing things are born out of problems that needed to be solved or weaknesses that needed to be overcome. Once you've recognized what your weaknesses are, begin to enact a plan to help yourself move past them or compensate for them. In my case, I had to work extra hard at baseball. I had to work harder than my teammates to compensate for not having two hands; I had to figure out how to transfer the ball and glove so I could both field cleanly and throw as quickly as all the guys with two hands. I also had to learn to hit the ball as hard as everyone else without the luxury of having two hands on the bat. I kept practicing, and I began to find ways to make up for my missing left hand. I had to keep problem solving to figure out how I could keep going.

I once heard a story about another guy who had a great weakness to overcome. His situation was far grimmer than mine. In 1947, a little boy and his parents received devastating news. News that no parent ever wants to hear. Six-year-old Ralph Braun was diagnosed with spinal muscular atrophy. This was a life-changing diagnosis; SMA is a rare genetic disorder that results in the loss of

129

motor neurons and causes muscle wasting. It can be so severe that it causes early death. The Braun family would never be the same.

By the time Ralph was 15, he was completely unable to walk, and he was too big for piggyback rides from his father. The doctors told him and his parents that he would never be independent. It would have been so easy for Ralph and his family to believe the doctors. But they didn't. Times were much different for people with disabilities in the 1950s. Ralph was desperate to be independent and desperate not to be institutionalized.

Ralph decided he was going to fight for his independence. As it turned out for him, necessity was indeed the mother of invention, and so while completely bound to his wheelchair, he invented his own motorized scooter to keep himself moving. Then he invented a wheelchair lift for an old jeep, complete with hand controls. For the first time, he could drive himself wherever he wanted.

In 1972 Ralph founded BraunAbility, a company that has since revolutionized life for people who need wheelchairs. Thousands of lives have been transformed with BraunAbility's wheelchair lifts and wheelchair vehicles. People all over the globe now have independence because of one man's determination—because one man decided to turn his weakness into a strength.

Ralph Braun could have handled his diagnosis and disability in a lot of different ways. But he chose to believe in the ability God gave him. He chose not to let the disability or limitations define him. He chose to be a problem solver and use his weakness for incredible good.

Ralph's parents instilled a will in him to overcome. And overcome he did. Ralph lived to be in his seventies, and his company continues to proudly carry on his legacy.4

Find Strength in Others

I think finding strength in others hearkens back to our team player chapter—you have to surround yourself with the right people. When you know you struggle in a certain area, part of the way you can help compensate for that is by building the right teams in your life.

The lack of my left hand is definitely not the only weakness I've struggled with. Organization is another one of my weaknesses. What comes naturally to others is completely foreign to me. My sweet fiancé finally set up a shared calendar for us because I was constantly springing events and plans on her at the last minute. And even with that, I've forgotten things. Keeping track of information, filing, writing down details—not my gift. This is an area I've had to really work to hone and discipline myself to improve upon. I have to stop and take the time to add things to my calendar, pass along the message, and file the important documents and e-mails. I've also learned that I can do what I do best when I'm surrounded by people who excel in areas where I am weak. Sometimes, our best move is to delegate as we are able and trust others who are better at certain skills. If it weren't for my mom and other organizers and board members on the NubAbility team, our camps would be pick-up kickball games in my dad's bean fields.

Whether it's business, ministry, sports, or even your personal relationships, I think there's wisdom in surrounding yourself with people who share your core values but who also have strengths in areas where you are weaker. Proverbs 27:17 (nlt) tells us, "As iron sharpens iron, so a friend sharpens a friend." This verse makes me both smile and cringe. It makes me smile because I think of how having the right people in our lives makes us sharper and more effective. It makes me cringe because the thought of iron clanking up against iron sounds painful and unpleasant. Sometimes, I think it is.

Have you ever had a teammate, coach, or a boss who challenged you in ways that were uncomfortable? Have you had people in your life who stretched you outside your comfort zone? Or frankly, sometimes ticked you off? Have you ever had a friend love you enough to tell you the truth about yourself? I have. It's not always pleasant. But when you have the right people sharpening you, it's worth it.

Did you know that when President Lincoln formed his cabinet, he appointed three men who ran against him in the 1860 Republican presidential nomination? Attorney General Edward Bates, Secretary of the Treasury Salmon P. Chase, and Secretary of State William H. Seward were all men who had opposed Lincoln. Historian Doris Kearns Goodwin documents this story and the history of Lincoln's entire cabinet in her 2005 book, Team of Rivals: The Political Genius of Abraham Lincoln. I think it takes a lot of wisdom and humility to acknowledge that even your rivals might have strengths you need in your life. President Lincoln was apparently not afraid of the clashing and clanking of iron to make him and his team more effective when the world could not afford for them to fail.

In an interview with the author, when asked why Lincoln believed he should fill his team with rivals, she responded:

"His explanation at the time was that these were the strongest men in the country. He declared that at a time of peril, the country needed to have the strongest men, and that he couldn't deprive it of those talents. . . . By putting his rivals in his cabinet, he had access to a wide range of opinions, which he realized would sharpen his own thinking. It also gave him a way of keeping all those conflicting opinions together. If he didn't have a unified group fighting against the South, the fight would be impossible to sustain. So having all those opinions in his cabinet not only helped him; it helped the country as well. . . . But it took an enormous amount of self-confidence. What he did was unprecedented at that time." 5

This wasn't easy; in fact, there was considerable friction, and they generally did not get along well. William Seward balked at accepting his nomination as secretary of state up to Lincoln's inauguration day. 6 In spite of this, though, he and Lincoln seemed to develop a relationship of friendship, trust, and support. Seward later said of his commander in chief: "Henceforth all men will come to see him as you and I have seen him —a true, loyal, patient, patriotic, and benevolent man." He added: "Abraham Lincoln will take his place with Washington and Franklin and Jefferson and Adams and Jackson, among the benefactors of the country and of the human race." 7

How often do we miss out on world-changing relationships because we're not brave enough to be friends with people who are different than we are? Whether you're in business or ministry or any kind of leadership position, be mindful of the team you are building around you. Don't be afraid to add people to your life who are stronger than you in certain areas. Wise leaders know how to help turn their weaknesses into strengths by surrounding themselves with the right people.

Sometimes, when we are facing one of our weaknesses or are unfortunately discovering a new one, what we really need is a little perspective. When I was a kid I was really impulsive and I was easily distracted. In addition to the emotional issues I was dealing with regarding having only one hand, I was also bouncing off the walls. I'm pretty sure this was mostly unrelated to having one hand. I think if I'd been born with two, I would have simply been bouncing off the walls and would have had two hands to cause trouble with. The only real connection point I can see is that I loved to make people laugh, and I also knew that if they were laughing at

133

something else, even if it was something that I caused, they wouldn't be laughing at my nub.

Needless to say, I caused some ruckuses for my teachers. One of my favorite things to do was sit in class and twist my thumb nubbin around and around until I could let it go and it would spin around like a helicopter. I always made sure that I had eye contact with the teacher when I did this. It was not their favorite thing. By the time fifth grade rolled around, my class clown act was starting to be less tolerated even by my peers. The kids were laughing less and judging more, and the teacher conferences with my parents became more serious. After a lot of discussion and prayer, my parents decided to have me tested for ADHD.

It was a surprise to no one when I was diagnosed with it. But what was a surprise was the way the news was delivered to me. My pediatrician literally asked my mom to step aside so he and I could have a talk. He told me that I had ADHD—Attention-Deficit Hyperactivity Disorder.

And then he said, "But I don't like calling it a disorder. I think God just made your order different. So instead of telling you what you can't do, I'm going to tell you all the things this means for you—all the things you'll be able to do because you have it. You see, some of the best emergency room doctors I know have ADHD. They can do multiple things of high importance at one time and focus on the priority." He continued. "You know, ADHD helped some of our presidents manage our nation. You'll be a sponge at learning about things you're interested in, and you'll be able to learn more than others. The only issue is that your eight-hour school day is set up more for kids who learn differently than you. But you can still do it; you just have to figure out your adaptations to maximize the best way to succeed."

That was one wise doctor. Though my family and I had to navigate medication and we had some tough times getting things figured out for me, I didn't leave that day feeling afraid, or like I was different, or like I had another weakness. It was almost like he told me I had a superpower. And I was like, "Cool, okay, I can do that."

Let God shift your perspective on what you think might be your weaknesses. In 2 Corinthians 12, Paul talks about this thorn in his flesh. We don't know exactly what it was, but based on how he shares about it, it seems to be some kind of weakness. In verses 8–12 (nlt), Paul said: "Three different times I begged the Lord to take it away. Each time he said, ``My grace is all you need. My power works best in weakness.' So now I am glad to boast about my weaknesses, so that the power of Christ can work through me. That's why I take pleasure in my weaknesses, and in the insults, hardships, persecutions, and troubles that I suffer for Christ. For when I am weak, then I am strong."

[[callout: My grace is all you need. My power works best in weakness. —2 Corinthians 12:9 nlt]]

Whatever your weakness happens to be, God has a good plan and purpose for you. Don't give up. When we become weak so He can be strong, He can turn our weaknesses into incredible strengths. Surrender them to him, and you might find out that our weaknesses are in fact superpowers in the hands of God.

Chapter 12
Remember, Life's a Dance, Not a Fight

Be Sure To Enjoy The Journey

"God does not give us overcoming life—He gives us life as we overcome."

Oswald Chambers, My Utmost for His Highest

In one of my final baseball games in high school, we played an away game that had a belligerent and ridiculous crowd. It was as if Facebook during an election year were happening in real life—in person for everyone to see and experience with a front-row seat. Only, I wasn't in a seat. I was on the mound, and I was the candidate everyone was hell-bent on crushing.

Coach put me in the game during the fourth inning, and I started out doing okay and throwing pretty hard and consistently. But then someone yelled out a remark about a one-handed pitcher. And then another. And another. Before I knew it, a crowd of adults was hurling insults my way. I was trying to keep it together, but it wasn't going so well. I was getting agitated and aggressive, and I was losing control.

My mom was sitting down the third baseline, out of earshot to what was happening. But she could tell by watching me pitch that something was wrong. She could only see my aggression and was getting annoyed at the way I was acting until her friend walked down the line to talk to her.

"Wow, Jana, I can't believe how well Sam is handling this," she said.

"How well he's handling what?" my mom replied, as she thought I was simply acting like a jerk because I was frustrated with how I was pitching (which, by the way, was not tolerated in the Kuhnert house.) Her friend went on to repeat some of the many insults that were being hurled at her son.

"Grown adults are making fun of him, Jana, because of his missing hand."

My dad wasn't there that night. It was rare for him to miss a game, but he had to be out in the fields, so he wasn't there to hear all the things that were said for himself. Later, Mom said it must have been God's way of keeping him from going to jail. Probably true, but I have to tell you, Mama Bear was none too happy either.

It was an unspoken rule around our high schools that the parents didn't come to the dugout or talk to the players during the game, but my mother broke that rule that night. When the inning was over, she called me over to her and practically grabbed ahold of me through the fence:

"You come here," she said. She sounded mad, but I knew she wasn't mad at me. "You will not let them win. You will have fun on that mound. You will go out there and strike them out, and you will not let them steal your joy." She let go of my jersey and stormed back to her seat. And I knew she was right. Her words snapped me out of my haze and reminded me of my dad's wisdom that he often says to me still to this day: life's a dance, not a fight.

I had been on that mound fighting. I was upset and agitated, and I had let those people into my head. Anytime I got into trouble on the mound, my dad always reminded me of that. Even with my pitching, it was a dance, not a fight. When we were done batting, I went back to the mound, and I got set to dance.

As you know, it took me a lot of years before I came to a place where I was okay enough with myself to put down my fists, shut my mouth (I still struggle with that one sometimes), and dance instead of fight. But I know enough by now to know that things pretty much always turn out better when I dance.

For our last game-changing practice, I want to encourage you to enjoy life and remember that it's a dance. You wouldn't necessarily think you have to practice enjoying life, but sometimes you actually do. The older I get, the more I understand how easy it can be to get bogged down into the stress of adulthood, to be angry about so many things. Instead, let's work at the practice of the dance—the practice of enjoying life to the fullest. In John 10:10, Jesus tells us, "I have come that they may have life, and have it to the full." niv

It took me a long time to learn these lessons, and I made a lot of mistakes along the way. I hope I can give you some practical tools that will help you take hold of these things a little faster than I did. I'll leave these here with you just in case I'm not around to grab you by the jersey and remind you about it next time you're put in a situation that makes you want to fight. Here are a few ways I learned to dance:

Let's Put Down Our Swords

There sure seems to be a lot of hate in this world. And it is really hard to dance if you're full of hate. I know. I used to be an angry kid. During that season of my life, I wasn't dancing or really enjoying life, and I wasn't making it too enjoyable for the people around me either.

I mentioned Facebook at the beginning of the chapter, and man, I wish I were joking about it, but I wasn't. Have you noticed how mean we've become as a society? Have you noticed how easily offended we are?

We hear a lot of stories about hate and offense. More and more often. Have you noticed when there's some type of tragedy, rather than a massive outpouring of empathy, we tend to see a massive outpouring of finger-pointing and blame? This is a deep and troubling part of our world, and I know there's a better way to live. All humans were created in the image of God. Whether they are missing a limb, or are a different color than you, or whatever, they deserve to be treated with kindness and respect. Even when people do really stupid things, does it really help anything when we all get mad about it on the Internet? Shame on us for being unkind and for shaming others. We all need to put down our swords. It's okay to be passionate, and it's okay to have a voice, but there's a difference in being full of hate and being passionate about something. I firmly believe that no one going through life who has a sword in hand and is constantly ready for combat will ever be able to enjoy the dance and make the most out of this journey. Here are some tips and habits on how to lay down our swords when the temptation to fight is coming at us:

1. When you're tempted to say too much on the Internet: Don't That's it. Seriously, what if we simply turned off the Internet and went to sleep? Don't write it. Don't DM it. Don't tweet it or retweet it. Don't share it. Don't post it. Don't fan the flames of anger. By "say too much," I'm talking about saying unkind things, shaming people, venting anger, arguing, and saying things carelessly without thinking them through—basically behaving like an Internet troll. I think we should apply this even to strangers and celebrity figures. It's like we all need to go back to what our mamas used to say: "If you can't say anything nice, don't say anything at all." Because we're all people. Our lives will be better if we can learn and choose to be kind, be silent, or use our voices for good in a way that is not shaming or condemning others.

And while you're at it—while you're busy at being kind to others on the Internet—be kind to yourself. Don't share things you'll regret. You are worth too much. It's funny to think that people not even a full generation of people older than me made it through their youths and early twenties without having have every mistake they've ever made eternally cemented on the world wide web. Think through every post and every photo. You never know when a prospective employer or future mother-in-law will be scanning your feed.

I've noticed there is no age limit on this advice. Whenever I'm about to say something publicly, on a stage or on the Internet, I ask myself some questions to make sure I'm really thinking through what I'm about to express. These might be some good questions to ask yourself: would I go back to my high school or college graduation, grab a microphone, and shout this from the stage? Would I wear those clothes while I was doing it? Would my family be proud of what's about to take place? Would I say this with me grandma is sitting in the front row? Rules to live by, people. Think of your grandma.

Another great time to apply this information is when you're responding to people via e-mail or text. Ever get really mad about something and type up an angry reply? Ever hit send? I have. And about five seconds after you hit the send button, you get the worst, sinking feeling in the pit of your stomach. Stop yourself. Write it in your journal. But do not send it.

The bottom line is this. I've met some amazing game changers, and they're full of kindness in person, online, and especially when no one in particular is watching. Let's be people like that.

2. Put yourself in other people's shoes. Strangely, this works both ways. You see, when Skater Dude spent the seventh grade terrorizing me, it would have been nice if he'd thought about what it

was like to be me. What it was like to be born without a hand. I bet he never took a minute to think about how hard so many things were for me for so long because I didn't get the opportunity to have two hands. And I bet while he was terrorizing me, he never stopped to be grateful he had two hands to tie his shoes, or clap his hands, or carry his books.

On the flip side, I probably could have tried to put myself in his shoes too. I can't know this for certain, but maybe there's a chance he wasn't growing up in the most stable or loving home. It's possible he didn't have parents at home who were as great as mine, or brothers who loved him as much as mine love me. Maybe he didn't actually have any confidence in himself or security in his life, so he took it out on me. If I had put myself in his shoes, I might have felt some compassion for him. And maybe I would have cared a little less about what he was saying to me. I see kids all the time who make me realize we just have no idea how much suffering is in this world. None at all. The Bible tells us to clothe ourselves with compassion. I think if every person who bears the name of Christ asked for His help to do that on a daily basis, it would transform the world. Before you allow yourself to be offended and before you reach for your sword, stop—even for a minute—and put yourself in the other person's shoes.

[[callout: Therefore, as God's chosen people, holy and dearly loved, clothe yourselves with compassion, kindness, humility, gentleness and patience. —Colossians 3:12 niv]]

We're so easily triggered and quick to fight these days. I'm not sure why that is. Maybe we spend too much time hiding behind screens. Maybe we need to spend more time sitting on porches together. More time holding hands. More time watching children play and holding sleeping puppies.

Before you get mad, take a deep breath. Put yourself in the other person's shoes. See if you can see things from their viewpoint.

And when you still absolutely can't see things from their vantage point, hold yourself to a higher standard anyway.

3. Sometimes you have to walk away. I once picked off a kid at first base during a game. The kid was a little cocky, and he was getting too big of a lead off the base. So I fired the ball to first and got him out. I thought he was a little cocky, well, his coach was a lot worse. He couldn't believe the kid had gotten thrown out by me, and he wasn't very kind about it. The coach actually came out on the field yelling, "There's no way that one-handed pitcher picked him off! It's a balk! It's a balk!"

In a world where I had been the umpire, I would have tossed that guy out of the game faster than the kid had been picked off of first base. But I wasn't the umpire. And my coach and the other responsible adults watching in despair weren't either. So when the man kept carrying on about the "one-handed pitcher" and the umpire continued to not do anything about it, my coach called all of my teammates and me off the field, and he packed us up and we left. That was that. We weren't going to hang around for this fight; it was nonsense, and my coach did the wise thing and walked away.

I hated that back then, and I still kind of hate this one now. I get it, but for me, this one is the hardest practice because it brings me face to face with the reality that I'm not in control. No matter what I hope or think I might be able to do, I can't control what other people choose. And that is a tough truth to swallow. We can choose to dance, but we can't make anyone else join us. In life, we all have moments where we've done everything to the best of our ability— we've been kind, we've been responsible, we've played by the rules, we've been compassionate—and sadly, things still might not turn out the way we hoped. I hate that, but I have to accept it. If you haven't had that experience yet, you will likely face it at some point.

When change isn't happening like you hoped, when people keep breaking promises, when someone is getting in your face, when the nonsense is getting out of control—the time will come when you'll have to walk away. It's a really difficult part of the dance, but in the long run, it's better than fighting forever. Pray over it. Seek wisdom, and know when it's time to walk away.

These three disciplines—being extremely careful what I say to people both in person and on the Internet, putting myself in other people's shoes, and knowing when to walk away—have really helped me. I hope they are helpful to you. We need more people on the dance floor and fewer people armed and ready to fight.

Remember, it's not about us. It's hard not to live life like it's all about me. I don't know about you, but I'm often the first person I think of when I wake up in the morning and the last one I think about before I go to bed. When I get ready to go on stage and speak, it's my face in the mirror I'm closely inspecting to make sure a small bit of lunch isn't still hanging out in my teeth. And I can honestly tell you; I'm not checking out other people's teeth before they go on stage.

It's so easy to be obsessively caught up with ourselves. It's part of our sinful nature, and it's a hard habit to break. Interestingly enough, the more we get over ourselves and focus on others, the happier our lives will be. One because there is joy in pouring our lives into others, and two because we're no longer obsessing about what other people think of us. I'm going to let you in on a secret, most of the time, people aren't actually thinking of us at all. Go back up a paragraph; just like we're always thinking about ourselves, so is pretty much everyone else.

I used to be so worried about what everyone thought about me and if they noticed my missing hand; thankfully, I don't really have a whole lot of extra time to care right now. I know what it's like to be worried about that, and I know now what it's like to spend my energy concerned with how I can help other kids and athletes achieve their best. The second is a much better use of my time.

143

Enjoy the Journey

How's that for a final practice to become a game changer? I want you to learn how to enjoy the journey.

In the game of baseball, we begin the journey—the ballgame—with the end in mind. We set out on the field with the intention of winning. Some people think baseball is a slow game, but it's wonderfully intricate and full of strategy. If you want to see a dance, watch how baseball players interact on the field.

Pitching in particular has a detailed plan in place. Baseball pitchers include starters, relievers, and closers. The hope is that a starter can carry you through to the end, but the reality is that that's a long time for an arm to hold. That's what makes no-hitters and perfect games rare and magnificent things to behold.

Because we know a starter can't always make it through, teams have an arsenal of relief pitchers. The name is pretty self-explanatory. They come in to offer relief. Maybe for half the game. Maybe for an inning or two. And then the closers. Think big, fierce, unhittable pitchers whose job it is to come in at the end of the game and wrap it up with a win. That's the plan. Go in and win; adapt and use what you have as you need it to achieve the primary goal.

When you think about it, that's kind of how life is. You declare your goal, make a plan and a couple back-up plans, and then adapt as needed. Always keep your eye on the goal, but don't forget this important piece—enjoy the process.

The thing is, if you don't enjoy playing the game of baseball, it's all rather pointless. Of course we can go in with the end in mind, we can work hard, and we can have a plan to execute and a back-up plan to adapt to, but if we're stressed and tense and we hate the whole process, well, that kind of stinks.

As I look back at my time playing baseball I think about how glad I am I got to play. Even during the hard times, and even when it was work, I loved it so much. A day came when I had to sit across from a doctor and be told that I was never going to play again. I had done some damage to my shoulder that unfortunately, was irreparable. It broke my heart. That day, I thought back to last game I played. It was one of the best games of my life, and later, my family saw a write-up about me in a Chattanooga newspaper near the university we played against. The article went into lengthy detail about my outing—the game I won—and how well I had pitched. It never once mentioned the fact that I was missing my hand. That was my dream—to be recognized as a great ball player—with no mention of my differences.

Think about what it might be like in heaven someday, looking back on our lives. The most important thing is that we know Jesus as our Savior and that we get there—in a matter of saying—that we win. And then from that vantage point, how will we view our lives? Did we also enjoy the game? Should we have relaxed a little bit more and not gotten so frustrated over small things? Should we have made more of a point to fully embrace the people that we love and squeeze every last drop of this beautiful life?

From heaven, I think we'll have a whole lot of perspective to analyze our earthly troubles and see how we could have been a little calmer about a whole lot of things. If you want to sweat about something, sweat about people knowing Jesus, about helping kids, about following His call on your life. And then let's relax a little more about some of the other things. Let's go out and experience our favorite things. Appreciate nature. Work hard at what we love. See the world. Watch the game. Eat the ice cream. Hug people. Let's pick good things and really make the most of them. Remember, Jesus came that we might have life and life to the full. Let's enjoy the game.

And finally, if you're alive and breathing, I want you to remember these three things:

Today is a gift, and life is full of opportunity. For you.
God has a plan and a purpose for you. For you.
I think somebody out there needs you. Yes, you.

     I hope you grab hold of these truths and take them to heart. I hope it makes you get out on the field and play the game, and in spite of the hard times that come to all of us, I hope you enjoy so much of it. I hope you have a rich and full game-changing life. I hope you get to look back on your life from heaven and see that with God's help, you played a great game and you made an impact on so many lives.

     You can do it, my friend. Don't be afraid when you can't see the next step. Trust me, you'll learn as you go, and God will never leave you. Put one foot in front of the other and just keep going. As we say at NubAbility:

Adapt
Overcome
Encourage
Believe and know that God is here, and He's got your back.

Wow, what a beautiful life it is.

Notes

"Pete Gray, Major Leaguer With One Arm, Dies at 87," New York Times, accessed October 10, 2018.
https://www.nytimes.com/2002/07/02/sports/pete-gray-major-leaguer-with-one-arm-dies-at-87.html

William C. Kashatus, One-Armed Wonder: Pete Gray, Wartime Baseball, and the American Dream (Jefferson, NC: McFarland & Company, Inc., Publishers, 1995), 126.

"One-Armed Pete Gray's Career Was Short and Bitter," Chicago Tribune, accessed October 10, 2018.
http://www.chicagotribune.com/news/ct-xpm-1989-04-20-8904050969-story.html

"Father of the Mobility Movement—Ralph Braun," Braunability, accessed October 10, 2018, https://www.braunability.com/ralph-braun/.

"An Extraordinary President and His Remarkable Cabinet: An interview with Doris Kearns Goodwin about Lincoln's Team of Rivals," National Archives, accessed October 10, 2018, https://www.archives.gov/publications/prologue/2006/spring/interview.html.

"Cabinet and Vice Presidents," Mr. Lincoln's White House, accessed October 10, 2018, http://www.mrlincolnswhitehouse.org/residents-visitors/cabinet-vice-presidents/.

John M. Taylor, William Henry Seward: Lincoln's Right Hand (New York: HarperCollins, 1991) 234.

About the Author

"I will not let your perception of my limits, limit my determination to crush your pity and replace it with your respect for my ability to compete."

Sam Kuhnert

Sam Kuhnert was born with one hand, but that has never stopped him from embracing God's purpose for him. When people used to ask Sam about his limb-difference, he'd smile and answer, "Because God said I didn't need an 'extra' hand!" Owning his difference made all the difference in his ability to move forward with confidence in sports, even after many said he'd never play outside of rec level.

For years, Sam dreamed of playing professional baseball. He trained hard, took extra lessons, and practiced pitching year-round, even when coaches told him he'd never make it, even when he was cut from his school team every year of middle school, and even when players on other teams mocked him relentlessly. His hard work paid off when he landed a college scholarship for his pitching. Sam knew he was on his way to becoming a baseball star, just as he had always prayed. But then a life-threatening illness and a bad injury ended his college career before Sam's graduation. Feeling lost, Sam turned to God in prayer and trusted as God walked him into his true purpose—a purpose God had planted in his heart years earlier.

At only 17 years old, Sam had a vision from God to create sports camps for kids like him. After his pro dreams were dashed, Sam poured himself into becoming the best possible head coach for

NubAbility Athletics Foundation, the sports camp organization he founded. NubAbility Athletics Foundation has exploded into a global non-profit charity that helps him teach thousands of children who have differences that they too can overcome challenges and live a triumphant purpose.

In 2017, Sam was named one of the ten Top Outstanding Young Americans. As the founder and coach of NubAbility Athletics Foundation and speaker, Sam spends every single day working with kids and making real changes in their lives. In addition to coaching and working with NubAbility, Sam continues to speak to people around the nation. God is using him to reach and encourage more kids in this capacity than he ever could have as a pro baseball player. His goal is to show kids how they can tap into God's purpose for them and become game changers for God too. Sam is engaged to the love of his life and resides in his hometown of DuQuoin, Illinois.

About NubAbility

The NubAbility® Athletics Foundation exists to encourage, inspire, instruct limb different youth (congenital or traumatic amputees) by getting them out of the stands, off the bench and into mainstream sports. Children are matched with coaches who have the same or similar limb differences. Since 2012, NubAbility has hosted more than 25 camps and has served more than 650 campers from around the world. Find out more at https://nubability.org/.

Made in the USA
Monee, IL
14 October 2021

79526677R10085